COOK'S KITCHEN

Traditional
Christmas
Recipes

igloobooks

Published in 2017
by Igloo Books Ltd
Cottage Farm
Sywell
NN6 0BJ
www.igloobooks.com

Food photography and recipe development © Stockfood, the Food Media Agency
Cover images © Stockfood, the Food Media Agency

STA002 0617
2 4 6 8 10 9 7 5 3
ISBN: 978-1-78440-808-4

Printed and manufactured in China

Contents

Christmas Buffet

Sausage Rolls

MAKES 16–20

PREPARATION TIME 20 MINUTES

COOKING TIME 18–22 MINUTES

INGREDIENTS

1 tbsp Worcestershire sauce
1 tbsp hot sauce
1 tbsp dried thyme
450 g / 1 lb / 3 cups sausage meat
salt and freshly ground black pepper
450 g / 1 lb ready-made puff pastry
a little plain (all-purpose) flour, for dusting
1 large egg, beaten
wholegrain mustard, to serve

METHOD

- Preheat the oven to 200°C (180°C fan) / 400F / gas 6 and grease and line a large baking tray with greaseproof paper.

- Combine the Worcestershire sauce, hot sauce, thyme, sausage meat and seasoning in a mixing bowl.

- Roll out the puff pastry on a lightly floured surface into a large rectangle, then split it in half lengthways.

- Arrange a layer of sausage meat mixture down the middle of each pastry rectangle, then brush each with beaten egg on one edge.

- Fold the other side of the pastry over onto the egg-washed edge.

- Press down to seal and trim away any excess. Cut some shallow slashes along each pastry roll, then cut each roll into 8–10 small sausage rolls.

- Place the sausage rolls on the baking tray, brush with beaten egg and bake for 18–22 minutes, until the pastry is crisp and golden and the sausage meat is cooked through.

- Serve with pots of wholegrain mustard.

TOP TIP

Replace the wholegrain mustard with other varieties, or try pickle instead.

Smoked Salmon Blinis

MAKES 18

PREPARATION TIME 20–25 MINUTES

COOKING TIME 20 MINUTES

INGREDIENTS

55 g / 2 oz / ⅓ cup buckwheat flour

110 g / 4 oz / ⅔ cup strong white plain (all-purpose) flour

¾ tsp salt

½ tsp baking powder

1 ½ tsp fast-action dried yeast

150 g / 5 oz / ⅔ cup crème fraiche

175 ml / 6 fl. oz / ¾ cup semi-skimmed milk

2 medium egg yolks

55 g / 2 oz / ¼ cup unsalted butter, melted

250 g / 9 oz / 1 cup sour cream

225 g / 8 oz / 1 ½ cups smoked salmon slices, roughly torn

a small handful of pickled gherkins in vinegar, drained

a few sprigs of dill, to garnish

1 lime, cut into wedges

salt and freshly ground black pepper

METHOD

- Prepare the blini batter by sifting together the flours, salt and baking powder into a large mixing bowl.

- Sprinkle the yeast on top, then combine the crème fraiche and milk in a saucepan and heat together gently over a low heat.

- Remove from the heat after a few minutes and whisk in the egg yolks until smooth.

- Pour over the flour mixture and whisk until smooth. Set to one side.

- Brush the base of a blini pan or frying pan with a little melted butter and heat it over a moderate heat until hot.

- Add small ladles of the batter to the pan and cook the blinis, three or four at a time, until set and golden underneath.

- Flip and cook the other sides for 1 minute, then transfer to a lined plate.

- Top the cooked blinis with spoons of sour cream and finely chop the gherkins before sprinkling on top.

- Fold and roll slices of the salmon, positioning them on top of the gherkins.

- Serve with a garnish of dill, some lime wedges and a little salt and pepper.

TOP TIP

Store leftover lemon or limes wedges in the freezer for next time.

Chicken Sesame Goujons

SERVES 8

PREPARATION TIME 15–20 MINUTES

COOKING TIME 9–12 MINUTES

INGREDIENTS

1 l / 1 pint 16 fl. oz / 4 cups vegetable oil, for deep-frying

4 large skinless chicken breasts

2 small egg whites

salt and freshly ground black pepper

250 g / 9 oz / 2 cups sesame seeds

250 ml / 9 fl. oz / 1 cup sweet chilli (chili) sauce, for dipping

METHOD

- Heat the oil in a large, heavy-based saucepan to 180°C / 350F.

- Place the chicken breasts between two sheets of greaseproof paper and flatten them out using a tenderiser or a rolling pin.

- Once flattened out and even in thickness, cut the breasts into large bite-sized pieces.

- Briefly whisk the egg whites with ½ tsp of salt in a mixing bowl until frothy and loose.

- Pat the chicken pieces dry and season with salt and pepper.

- Dip the pieces into the egg whites, then dredge in the sesame seeds to coat and arrange them on a wire rack.

- Deep-fry the chicken in batches for 3–4 minutes until golden and crisp, then flip them over halfway through frying.

- Drain on kitchen paper and serve warm with pots of chilli sauce for dipping.

TOP TIP

Skewer the finished chicken goujons with decorative cocktail sticks to serve.

Mushroom Vol-au-vents

MAKES 24

PREPARATION TIME 25 MINUTES

COOKING TIME 6–8 MINUTES

INGREDIENTS

450 g / 1 lb / 6 cups mixed wild mushrooms,
    brushed clean
2 tbsp unsalted butter
1 tbsp olive oil
2 shallots, finely chopped
2 cloves of garlic, minced
75 ml / 3 fl. oz / ⅓ cup double (heavy) cream
a small bunch of flat-leaf parsley,
    finely chopped
salt and freshly ground black pepper
24 vol-au-vent cases
a large handful of thyme sprigs, to garnish

METHOD

- Preheat the oven to 180°C (160°C fan) / 350F / gas 4 and line a large baking tray with a sheet of greaseproof paper.

- Roughly chop the mushrooms and set them to one side.

- Melt together the butter and oil in a large sauté pan set over a medium heat until hot.

- Add the shallots, garlic and a pinch of salt, sweating them steadily for 5–6 minutes.

- Increase the heat a little and add the mushrooms and a little more salt.

- Sauté for 6–7 minutes until the mushrooms are tender and starting to brown.

- Add the cream and parsley and stir to coat, seasoning to taste with salt and pepper.

- Fill the vol-au-vent cases with the mushroom mixture and arrange them on the lined baking tray.

- Bake in the oven for 6–8 minutes until warmed through.

- Remove and serve with a sprig of thyme on top.

TOP TIP

Garnish with parsley if thyme sprigs are unavailable.

Cheese Straws

MAKES 24

PREPARATION TIME 15 MINUTES

COOKING TIME 10–12 MINUTES

INGREDIENTS

350 g / 12 oz ready-made puff pastry
a little plain (all-purpose) flour, for dusting
55 g / 2 oz / ¼ cup unsalted butter, melted
150 g / 5 oz / 1 ½ cups Cheddar, finely grated
1 tsp hot paprika
½ tsp cumin seeds, lightly crushed

METHOD

- Preheat the oven to 220°C (200°C fan) / 425F / gas 7 and line a large baking tray with greaseproof paper.
- Roll out the pastry on a lightly floured surface into a square about 5 mm (½ in) thick.
- Trim the edges and discard the excess pastry.
- Cut the square in half, then brush with melted butter and sprinkle over the grated Cheddar, paprika and cumin onto both pieces.
- Cut each piece into straw shapes, approximately 1 cm (½ in) wide and arrange on the baking tray.
- Pinch the ends and twist the straws in opposite directions to shape them into braids.
- Bake for 10–12 minutes until risen and golden.
- Remove the straws to a wire rack to cool before serving.

TOP TIP
Use smoked paprika for a less intense spice.

CHRISTMAS BUFFET

Stuffed Peppadews

SERVES 4–6

PREPARATION TIME 15 MINUTES

CHILLING TIME 30 MINUTES

INGREDIENTS

1 large clove of garlic, minced

a small handful of chives, finely chopped

400 g / 14 oz / 2 cups cream cheese, softened

salt and freshly ground black pepper

450 g / 1 lb / 3 cups preserved peppadews in oil, drained

a few sprigs of coriander (cilantro), to garnish

METHOD

- Pulse together the garlic, chives, cream cheese and seasoning in a food processor until smooth.
- Scrape the filling into a piping bag fitted with a round nozzle.
- Pipe the cream cheese filling into the peppadews and chill for 30 minutes until firm.
- Serve with a garnish of coriander.

TOP TIP

Try using finely chopped spring onions (scallions) instead of chives.

Celeriac Remoulade

SERVES 4

PREPARATION TIME 15 MINUTES

INGREDIENTS

150 g / 5 oz / ⅔ cup plain yoghurt
75 g / 3 oz / ⅓ cup mayonnaise
1 lemon, juiced
a dash of Worcestershire sauce
a pinch of paprika
salt and freshly ground black pepper
2 large carrots, peeled
2 small celeriac, peeled
a small black truffle, shaved
a large handful of mixed herbs, to garnish

METHOD

- Whisk together the yoghurt, mayonnaise, lemon juice, Worcestershire sauce, paprika and seasoning in a large mixing bowl.
- Finely grate the carrots on a mandolin fitted with a julienne setting, then julienne the celeriac.
- Add the julienned vegetables to the sauce and stir well to combine.
- Add the black truffles and stir again briefly.
- Spoon into glasses and garnish with mixed herbs before serving.

TOP TIP
Crusty bread would make a tasty accompaniment to this dish.

Beef Empanadas

SERVES 8

PREPARATION TIME 45 MINUTES

COOKING TIME 20 MINUTES

INGREDIENTS

100 g / 3 ½ oz / ½ cup butter, cubed and chilled
200 g / 7 oz / 1 ⅓ cups plain (all-purpose) flour
2 tbsp olive oil
1 onion, finely chopped
1 red pepper, diced
1 red chilli (chili), finely chopped
2 cloves of garlic, crushed
½ tsp Cayenne pepper
225 g / 8 oz / 1 cup minced beef
200 ml / 7 fl. oz / ¾ cup beef stock
1 egg, beaten

METHOD

- First make the pastry. Rub the butter into the flour until the mixture resembles fine breadcrumbs. Stir in just enough cold water to bring the pastry together into a pliable dough then chill for 30 minutes.
- Heat the oil in a large saucepan and fry the onion, pepper and chilli for 3 minutes, stirring occasionally. Add the garlic and Cayenne and cook for 2 minutes, then add the mince. Fry the mince until it starts to brown, then add the stock and simmer for 20 minutes. Leave to cool completely.
- Preheat the oven to 200°C (180°C fan) / 400F / gas 6.
- Divide the pastry into 8 pieces and roll each piece out into a circle. Drain the filling of any excess liquid, then spoon it onto the pastry circles.
- Fold the pastries in half to enclose the filling then crimp round the edges to seal. Brush the pastries with the beaten egg.
- Bake the turnovers for 20 minutes or until the pastry is cooked through and crisp underneath.

TOP TIP
Brush a little of the beaten egg around the edges of the pastry, then fold.

Goats' Cheese and Pesto Puffs

MAKES 18

PREPARATION TIME 20 MINUTES

COOKING TIME 15 MINUTES

INGREDIENTS

700 g / 1 ½ lb / 3 ½ cups all-butter puff pastry
100 ml / 3 ½ fl. oz / ½ cup pesto
150 g / 5 ½ oz / 1 cup white-rinded goats'
    cheese, cubed
1 egg, beaten

METHOD

- Preheat the oven to 220°C (200°C fan) / 430F / gas 7.
- Roll out the pastry on a lightly floured surface and cut it into 12 rectangles. Top each rectangle with a spoonful of pesto and a few cubes of goat's cheese, then brush round the edges with beaten egg.
- Fold the pastries in half and press the edges firmly to seal.
- Brush the pastries with beaten egg and bake for 15 minutes or until golden brown and cooked through.

TOP TIP
Try other varieties of cheese, such as mozzarella or feta.

Individual Cheese and Onion Quiches

MAKES 6

PREPARATION TIME 30 MINUTES

COOKING TIME 35 MINUTES

INGREDIENTS

225 g / 8 oz / 1 cup all-butter puff pastry
2 tbsp butter
1 large onion, quartered and sliced
3 large eggs, beaten
225 ml / 8 fl. oz / 1 cup double (heavy) cream
150 g / 5 ½ oz / 1 ½ cups Gruyère, grated
salt and freshly ground black pepper

METHOD

- Preheat the oven to 190°C (170°C fan) / 375 F / gas 5.
- Roll out the pastry on a floured surface and use it to line a 6-hole cupcake tin.
- Heat the butter in a frying pan and fry the onion for 10 minutes to soften.
- Whisk the eggs with the double cream until smoothly combined then stir in the onions and half of the Gruyère. Season generously with salt and pepper.
- Pour the filling into the pastry cases and scatter the rest of the Gruyère on top.
- Bake for 25 minutes or until the pastry is cooked through and the filling is just set in the centre.

TOP TIP
Many types of cheese will work with this dish – why not try different varieties?

Florentines

METHOD

- Preheat the oven to 180°C (160°C fan) / 350°F / gas 4 and grease and line a large baking tray with greaseproof paper.

- Heat together the sugar, butter, cream and honey in a large saucepan set over a moderate heat.

- Remove the saucepan from the heat and stir through the almonds, flour, mixed peel and cherries.

- Leave the mixture to cool for 15 minutes, then take tablespoons of the mixture and spoon mounds onto the prepared tray.

- Flatten the mounds with a wetted finger and bake for 10–12 minutes until golden on top.

- Remove the tray from the oven and leave to cool on a wire rack.

- Melt together the chocolate and glucose in a heatproof bowl set over a half-filled saucepan of simmering water.

- Stir until melted, then remove from the heat.

- Carefully peel away the Florentines from the tray and dip their undersides in the melted chocolate.

- Place the dipped Florentines, chocolate-side facing up, on a wire rack and chill for 15 minutes.

- The Florentines are ready to serve once the chocolate has set.

MAKES 24

PREPARATION TIME 40–45 MINUTES

COOKING TIME 10–12 MINUTES

INGREDIENTS

175 g / 6 oz / ¾ cup caster (superfine) sugar
110 g / 4 oz / ½ cup unsalted butter, cubed
75 ml / 3 fl. oz / ⅓ cup double (heavy) cream
2 tbsp honey
300 g / 10 ½ oz / 2 ½ cups flaked (slivered) almonds
2 tbsp plain (all-purpose) flour
2 tbsp chopped mixed peel
75 g / 3 oz / ½ cup glacé cherries, chopped
300 g / 10 ½ oz / 2 cups dark chocolate, chopped
1 tsp liquid glucose

TOP TIP

Try using milk chocolate for a less intense chocolate taste.

Mini Meringues

MAKES 8

PREPARATION TIME 15–20 MINUTES

COOKING TIME 1 HOUR 45 MINUTES

INGREDIENTS

4 medium egg whites, at room temperature
a pinch of salt
a pinch of cream of tartar
225 g / 8 oz / 1 cup caster (superfine) sugar

METHOD

- Preheat the oven to 140°C (120°C fan) / 275F / gas and grease and line two baking trays with greaseproof paper.
- Beat the egg whites with a pinch of salt in a large mixing bowl until softly peaked.
- Add the cream of tartar and beat briefly, then beat in the sugar, 1 tbsp at a time, until the meringue is thick and glossy.
- Spoon mounds of the meringue onto the lined baking trays, spaced apart.
- Bake for 1 hour 45 minutes until dry, but not browned. The meringues should sound hollow when tapped on their undersides.
- Remove to a wire rack to cool before serving.

TOP TIP
Swirl food dye into the mix to give the meringues a different look.

White Chocolate Truffles

MAKES 36

PREPARATION TIME 3 HOURS 25 MINUTES

COOKING TIME 5–10 MINUTES

INGREDIENTS

600 g / 1 lb 5 oz / 4 cups good-quality white chocolate, chopped

400 ml / 14 fl. oz / 1 ¾ cups double (heavy) cream

75 g / 3 oz / ⅓ cup unsalted butter

a little sunflower oil

125 g / 4 ½ oz / 1 cup icing (confectioners') sugar, sifted

a pinch of food glitter, to garnish

METHOD

- Place the chocolate in a large heatproof mixing bowl.

- Warm together the cream and butter in a saucepan set over a medium heat. Stir until the butter has melted, then increase the heat and cook until almost boiling.

- Pour the hot cream over the chocolate and leave it to stand for 1 minute.

- Stir gently until the chocolate has melted evenly into the cream, then cover and chill for 3 hours until set but not too firm.

- Remove the mixture from the fridge and use a melon baller to remove scoops from the bowl.

- Using lightly oiled hands, roll the scoops into balls and arrange them on a lined baking tray.

- Roll the truffles in the icing sugar to coat, then arrange back on the tray and chill for 10 minutes.

- Let the truffles stand at room temperature for 10 minutes before serving with a pinch of glitter on top.

TOP TIP

Truffles make great gifts; seal into confectionery bags and tie with gold ribbon.

Hazelnut Profiteroles with Pear Sorbet

SERVES 6

PREPARATION TIME 1 HOUR 15 MINUTES

COOKING TIME 20 MINUTES

INGREDIENTS

55 g / 2 oz / ¼ cup butter, cubed

75 g / 2 ½ oz / ½ cup strong white bread
   flour, sieved

2 large eggs, beaten

3 tbsp hazelnuts (cobnuts), chopped

100 ml / 3 ½ fl. oz / ½ cup double
   (heavy) cream

1 tbsp Poire William liqueur

100 g / 3 ½ oz / ¾ cup dark chocolate
   (minimum 60% cocoa solids), chopped

600 ml / 1 pint / 2 ½ cups pear sorbet

METHOD

- Preheat the oven to 200°C (180°C fan) / 400F / gas 6. Line a baking tray with greaseproof paper and spray with a little water.

- Melt the butter with 150 ml / 5 fl. oz / ²/₃ cup water and bring to the boil. Immediately beat in the flour, off the heat, with a wooden spoon until it forms a smooth ball of pastry. Incorporate the egg a little at a time to make a glossy paste.

- Spoon the pastry into a piping bag fitted with a large plain nozzle and pipe 2.5 cm (1 in) buns onto the baking tray, then sprinkle with chopped hazelnuts.

- Bake for 20 minutes, increasing the temperature to 220°C (200°C fan) / 425F / gas 7 halfway through. Transfer the choux buns to a wire rack and make a hole in the underneath of each one so the steam can escape. Leave to cool completely.

- Heat the cream and liqueur to simmering point then pour it over the chocolate and stir to emulsify.

- Cut the choux buns in half and fill with sorbet, then serve 3 per person, drizzled with chocolate sauce.

TOP TIP

You could use ice cream instead of sorbet; try chocolate or caramel.

Peanut Millionaire's Shortbread

MAKES 6
PREPARATION TIME 20 MINUTES
COOKING TIME 3 HOURS 20 MINUTES
CHILLING TIME 20 MINUTES

INGREDIENTS

400 g / 14 oz can of condensed milk
150 g / 5 ½ oz / 1 cup salted peanuts
200 g / 7 oz dark chocolate (minimum
    70% cocoa solids), chopped
50 g / 1 ¾ oz / ½ cup butter

FOR THE SHORTBREAD
225 g / 8 oz / 1 ½ cups plain (all-purpose) flour
75 g / 2 ½ oz / ⅓ cup caster (superfine) sugar
150 g / 5 oz / ⅔ cup butter, cubed

METHOD

- Make the caramel layer in advance. Put the unopened can of condensed milk in a saucepan of water and simmer for 3 hours, adding more water as necessary to ensure it doesn't boil dry. Leave the can to cool completely.

- Preheat the oven to 180°C (160°C fan) / 350 F / gas 4 and line a 20 cm (8 in) square cake tin with greaseproof paper.

- To make the shortbread, mix together the flour and sugar in a bowl, then rub in the butter.

- Knead gently until the mixture forms a smooth dough then press it into the bottom of the tin in an even layer.

- Bake the shortbread for 20 minutes, turning the tray round halfway through. Leave to cool.

- Open the can of condensed milk and beat the caramel until smooth. Fold in the peanuts then spread it over the shortbread and chill for 1 hour.

- Put the chocolate and butter in a bowl set over a pan of simmering water and stir together until melted and smooth.

- Pour the mixture over the caramel layer and leave to cool and set before cutting into 6 bars.

TOP TIP
Sprinkle extra chopped peanuts over the top before chilling.

Apple, Raspberry and Marzipan Puffs

MAKES 20

PREPARATION TIME 20 MINUTES

COOKING TIME 15 MINUTES

INGREDIENTS

400 g / 14 oz / 1 ¾ cups ready-to-roll
    puff pastry
150 g / 5 ½ oz / ½ cup marzipan, sliced
1 apple, cored and thinly sliced
300 g / 10 ½ oz / 2 cups raspberries
1 egg, beaten

METHOD

- Preheat the oven to 220°C (200°C fan) / 425F / gas 7.

- Roll out the pastry on a lightly floured surface, then cut out 20 circles with a fluted pastry cutter.

- Lay a slice of marzipan, a slice of apple and 3 raspberries on top of each one, then brush the edge with egg. Fold over the pastry circles to enclose the filling and press the edges firmly to seal.

- Transfer the pastries to a non-stick baking tray and bake for 15 minutes or until the pastry is cooked through.

TOP TIP
Serve with fresh whipped cream as an optional extra.

Mulled Wine

SERVES 8

PREPARATION TIME 10 MINUTES

COOKING TIME 40–45 MINUTES

INGREDIENTS

1 tsp cloves
3–4 star anise
2 bay leaves
2 tsp green cardamom pods
5 cm (2 in) piece of cinnamon stick
125 g / 4 ½ oz / ½ cup caster (superfine) sugar
1 orange, cut into slices
1 tbsp dried cherries
1.5 l / 2 pints 12 fl. oz / 6 cups medium-
    bodied red wine

METHOD

- Heat a large saucepan over a moderate heat until hot.
- Add the spices and dry-fry for 30 seconds or until fragrant.
- Add the sugar, fruit and half of the wine, stirring well to combine.
- Bring the liquid to a simmer, stirring from time to time, until the sugar has completely dissolved.
- Add the remaining wine and return to a gentle simmer.
- Let the wine simmer for 40–45 minutes to allow the taste to develop and meld.
- Ladle the mulled wine into mugs and serve.

TOP TIP
Add a slice of orange to the glass and serve to your guests on arrival.

Eggnog Snowballs

MAKES 6–8

PREPARATION TIME 15–20 MINUTES

COOKING TIME 20–25 MINUTES

CHILLING TIME 3 HOURS

INGREDIENTS

4 medium egg yolks
85 g / 3 ½ oz / ⅓ cup caster (superfine) sugar
600 ml / 1 pint 2 fl. oz / 2 ½ cups whole milk
250 ml / 9 fl. oz / 1 cup double (heavy) cream
2 tsp freshly grated nutmeg
100 ml / 3 ½ fl. oz / ½ cup bourbon
2 medium egg whites
a pinch of salt
a few cinnamon sticks, to garnish

METHOD

- Beat together the egg yolks and 75 g / 3 oz / ¼ cup of the sugar in a heatproof mixing bowl until pale and thick.

- Combine the milk, cream and half the nutmeg in a saucepan set over a medium heat and warm until the mixture starts to boil.

- Remove it from the heat and gradually whisk into the egg yolks and sugar.

- Strain the mixture back into a clean saucepan and cook over a medium heat, stirring constantly, until it registers 72°C / 162F on a sugar thermometer.

- Stir through the bourbon and let the mixture cool slightly.

- Pour into a clean bowl, cover and chill the eggnog for 3 hours until cold.

- Once cold, beat the egg whites with a pinch of salt until softly peaked.

- Add the remaining sugar and continue to beat until thick and stiff.

- Whisk the egg whites into the chilled eggnog mixture.

- Ladle into glasses and garnish with freshly grated nutmeg and cinnamon sticks.

TOP TIP
Serve with ginger biscuits for an extra taste of Christmas spice.

Christmas Eve

Smoked Mackerel Pâté

SERVES 4

PREPARATION TIME 10–15 MINUTES

INGREDIENTS

450 g / 1 lb / 3 cups smoked mackerel
    fillets, cooked
100 g / 3 ½ oz / ½ cup plain yoghurt
100 g / 3 ½ oz / ½ cup cream cheese
½ lemon, juiced
2 tbsp olive oil
a small handful of Kalamata olives,
    pitted and chopped
salt and freshly ground black pepper
slices of white bread, to serve

METHOD

- Peel any skin from the mackerel fillets and discard any bone.
- Flake the fillets and add to a food processor along with the yoghurt, cream cheese, lemon juice, olive oil and olives.
- Blitz until the mixture comes together into a rough pâté-like, thick texture.
- Season to taste with plenty of salt and pepper.
- Spoon into pots, cover and chill until needed.
- Toast slices of the bread and serve alongside the pâté.

TOP TIP

Caramelised red onion chutney makes a tasty accompaniment to this pâté.

Tomato and Leek Soup

SERVES 4

PREPARATION TIME 15 MINUTES

COOKING TIME 40 MINUTES

INGREDIENTS

2 tbsp olive oil
2 leeks, finely chopped
2 cloves of garlic, crushed
1 tbsp concentrated tomato purée
400 g / 14 oz / 2 cups ripe tomatoes, chopped
1 litre / 1 pint 15 fl. oz / 4 cups vegetable stock
2 tbsp flat leaf parsley, chopped
salt and freshly ground black pepper

METHOD

- Heat the oil in a large saucepan. Reserve 2 tbsp of the leek for a garnish and stir the rest into the oil with the garlic. Season with salt and pepper, then cook over a low heat for 10 minutes, stirring occasionally.

- Stir in the tomato purée, tomatoes and stock, then cover and simmer for 30 minutes.

- Transfer the soup to a liquidiser and blend until smooth, then pass the soup through a sieve to remove any seeds and bits of skin.

- Taste for seasoning then ladle the soup into warm bowls. Mix the reserved leek with the parsley and sprinkle on top.

TOP TIP
Serve with crusty bread to dip into this classic soup.

Mushroom Soufflés

SERVES 4

PREPARATION TIME 25–30 MINUTES

COOKING TIME 18–22 MINUTES

INGREDIENTS

110 g / 4 oz / ½ cup butter, softened
2 tbsp olive oil
300 g / 10 ½ oz / 4 cups mixed wild
    mushrooms, brushed clean
75 g / 3 oz / ½ cup plain (all-purpose)
    flour, sifted
500 ml / 18 fl. oz / 2 cups whole milk
4 large egg yolks
150 g / 5 oz / 1 ½ cups Cheddar, grated
salt and freshly ground black pepper
4 large egg whites

METHOD

- Preheat the oven to 200°C (180°C fan) / 400F / gas 6.

- Brush the insides of four individual ramekins with 1 ½ tbsp of softened butter. Chill until needed.

- Heat the oil in a large sauté pan set over a moderate heat until hot.

- Sauté the mushrooms with a little seasoning for 4–5 minutes until softened and starting to brown.

- Scrape the mushrooms into a food processor and pulse until paste-like in texture. Set to one side.

- Melt the remaining butter in a saucepan set over a medium heat, then whisk in the flour, cooking for 2 minutes until golden and smooth.

- Add the milk in a slow, steady stream, whisking simultaneously, until fully incorporated.

- Whisk in the egg yolks and Cheddar and simmer for 5–6 minutes, stirring from time to time.

- Fold through the mushroom paste and season the mixture with salt and pepper.

- Beat the egg whites in a clean mixing bowl with a pinch of salt until softly peaked.

- Whisk one third of the egg whites into the soufflé batter before gently folding through the remainder.

- Divide between the ramekins and run the tip of a finger around the insides of the rims.

- Bake for 18–22 minutes until golden and risen before serving.

Roast Ham with Marmalade Glaze

SERVES 8–10

PREPARATION TIME 15 MINUTES

COOKING TIME 3 HOURS 10–15 MINUTES

INGREDIENTS

3 kg / 8 lb gammon joint

125 g / 4 ½ oz / ½ cup marmalade

2 oranges, sliced

4 ripe apricots, stoned and halved

75 g / 3 oz / ¾ cup cranberries

2 fresh bay leaves

100 g / 3 ½ oz / 2 cups mixed leaf salad,

75 ml / 3 fl. oz / ⅓ cup French vinaigrette,
    to serve

salt and freshly ground black pepper

METHOD

- Place the gammon in a large saucepan of water and heat over a moderate heat.
- Once boiling, drain the gammon well.
- Return the gammon to the saucepan and cover with enough water to submerge it.
- Heat the water until boiling, then reduce to a simmer for 2 hours.
- Drain well and leave to one side until cool enough to handle.
- Preheat the oven to 180°C (160°C fan) / 350F / gas 4.
- Lightly score a diamond pattern on top of the gammon with a sharp knife. Smear with marmalade and sit the gammon in a large roasting tin, sat on top of a trivet.
- Top the gammon with orange slices, apricots, cranberries and bay leaves.
- Roast for 45–50 minutes until the fruit is soft and the inside of the ham reaches at least 71°C / 160F on a meat thermometer.
- Remove the ham from the oven and serve warm or cold with salad and dressing on the side.

TOP TIP

Stud the gammon with whole cloves before roasting; remove before serving.

Pot-roasted Pork with Apples

SERVES 8
PREPARATION TIME 20 MINUTES
COOKING TIME 1 HOUR 30 MINUTES

INGREDIENTS

1.5 kg / 3 lb 3 oz / 8 cups pork loin joint
3 tbsp olive oil
4 cloves of garlic, roughly chopped
3 eating apples, cored and sliced
300 ml / 10 ½ fl. oz / 1 ¼ cups cider
2 tbsp flat leaf parsley, finely chopped
salt and black pepper

METHOD

- Preheat the oven to 180°C (160°C fan) / 350F / gas 4 and season the pork well with salt and pepper.
- Heat the oil in a cast iron casserole dish and sear the pork on all sides.
- Remove the pork from the pan, then fry the garlic and apples for 5 minutes. Season to taste with salt and pepper.
- Return the pork to the pot, then pour in the cider and bring to a simmer.
- Put on a lid, transfer it to the oven and pot-roast for 1 hour.
- Remove the lid, then return to the oven for 30 minutes.
- Leave to rest for 10 minutes, then sprinkle with parsley and serve.

TOP TIP
Apple sauce is the perfect accompaniment to roasted pork.

Venison Casserole

SERVES 4–6

PREPARATION TIME 25–30 MINUTES

COOKING TIME 1 HOUR 25–30 MINUTES

INGREDIENTS

2 tbsp sunflower oil

4 rashers of streaky bacon, chopped

750 g / 1 kg 10 oz / 5 cups boneless venison shoulder, diced

salt and freshly ground black pepper

3 tbsp unsalted butter

1 shallot, finely chopped

5 cm (2 in) piece of cinnamon stick

1 tbsp tomato purée

1 tbsp plain (all-purpose) flour

100 ml / 3 ½ fl. oz / ½ cup red wine

750 ml / 1 pint 6 fl. oz / 3 cups beef stock

450 g / 1 lb / 3 cups white potatoes, peeled and diced into small cubes

150 g / 5 oz / 1 cup seedless white grapes

2 tbsp walnut pieces

a few bay leaves

1 small orange

a pinch of crushed red peppercorns

METHOD

- Heat the oil in a large casserole dish set over a moderate heat until hot. Sauté the bacon for 2–3 minutes until golden, then remove from the dish.

- Season the venison with salt and pepper and seal in batches, removing to a plate when ready.

- Reduce the heat a little and add 1 tbsp of butter. Once melted, add the shallot and cinnamon, sautéing for 3–4 minutes.

- Stir through the tomato purée and cook for 1 minute. Stir in the flour.

- Cook for a further minute over a slightly reduced heat, then return the venison and bacon to the dish, stirring well.

- Increase the heat and cover the venison with the wine and stock. Once the liquid is boiling, reduce it to a simmer and half-cover the dish with a lid.

- Simmer for 1 hour 20–30 minutes until the venison is tender, stirring occasionally.

- Once the venison is ready, adjust the seasoning to taste and keep the casserole warm over a low heat.

- Melt the remaining butter in a large sauté pan set over a moderate heat.

- Add the potato and seasoning, then sauté for 1 minute and cover with a lid. Cook for 5–6 minutes, until the potato is soft.

- Remove the lid and continue to sauté for a few minutes until browned and crisp at the edges.

- Garnish the casserole with grapes, walnuts and bay leaves.

- Peel some fresh orange zest over the casserole and serve with the sautéed potatoes and a pinch of crushed red peppercorns.

Roast Chicken with Carrots

SERVES 4

PREPARATION TIME 10 MINUTES

COOKING TIME 1 HOUR 10 MINUTES

INGREDIENTS

1.5 kg / 3 lb 5 oz / 6 cups chicken
3 tbsp olive oil
450 g / 1 lb / 2 cups small rainbow
    carrots, scrubbed
1 lemon, halved
1 tbsp flat leaf parsley, chopped
salt and black pepper

METHOD

- Preheat the oven to 200°C (180°C fan) / 400F / gas 6.

- Season the chicken all over with sea salt and black pepper, then drizzle with olive oil and lay it breast side down in a large roasting tin.

- Transfer the tin to the oven and roast for 30 minutes.

- Turn the chicken breast side up and surround it with the carrots. Turn the carrots to coat them in the juices then roast for a further 40 minutes.

- To test if the chicken is cooked, insert a skewer into the thickest part of the thigh. If the juices run clear with no trace of blood, it is ready.

- Squeeze over the lemon halves and sprinkle with parsley before serving.

TOP TIP

Store any leftover chicken in the fridge and consume within three days.

Salmon Stuffed with Couscous

SERVES 12

PREPARATION TIME 20 MINUTES

COOKING TIME 40–45 MINUTES

INGREDIENTS

2 tbsp unsalted butter
250 g / 9 oz / 1 ½ cups couscous
2.75 kg / 6 lb salmon, gutted and skinned
salt and freshly ground black pepper
2 tbsp olive oil
a small handful of curly parsley, chopped
a large bunch of dill, roughly chopped
2 lemons
2 clementines
plain yoghurt, to serve

METHOD

- Preheat the oven to 180°C (160°C fan) / 425F / gas 4.
- Melt the butter in a saucepan set over a medium heat, then add the couscous and lightly fry for 1–2 minutes, stirring occasionally, until toasted.
- Cover the couscous with 1 cm (½ in) of boiling water and remove the pan from the heat. Cover with a lid and set to one side for 10 minutes.
- Meanwhile, wash and thoroughly dry the salmon, removing the head if attached. Sit the salmon on a sheet of greaseproof paper and lift it into a large roasting tray.
- Season the inside of the salmon with salt and pepper and drizzle it with olive oil.
- Fluff the couscous with a fork and stir through most of the chopped herbs and some seasoning.
- Fill the cavity of the salmon with the couscous and bring the greaseproof paper up and around the salmon.
- Grate the zest from the citrus fruit and set it to one side as a garnish, then cut the fruit in half and position inside the roasting tray.
- Place the tray in the oven and cook for 45–55 minutes until the fish is just cooked through.
- Remove from the oven and leave to rest for 10 minutes, then open and serve with a garnish of the remaining herbs and the citrus zest. Serve with yoghurt on the side.

Mushroom, Pea and Leek Filo Pies

SERVES 4

PREPARATION TIME 30 MINUTES

COOKING TIME 15 MINUTES

INGREDIENTS

2 tbsp olive oil

1 large leek, chopped

2 cloves of garlic, crushed

250 g / 9 oz / 3 ⅓ cups button
    mushrooms, quartered

100 g / 3 ½ oz / ⅔ cup peas, defrosted
    if frozen

100 ml / 3 ½ fl. oz / ½ cup dry white wine

8 sheets filo pastry

50 g / 1 ¾ oz / ¼ cup butter, melted

salt and freshly ground black pepper

METHOD

- Heat the oil in a frying pan and fry the leek and garlic for 5 minutes without browning.

- Add the mushrooms to the pan and season with salt and pepper, then cook for 10 minutes, stirring occasionally.

- Add the peas and wine and bubble until reduced by half. Season to taste with salt and pepper.

- Preheat the oven to 200°C (180°C fan) / 400F / gas 6.

- Divide the filling between 4 small pie dishes. Brush the filo with melted butter, then scrunch up the sheets and lay them on top.

- Bake the pies for 15 minutes or until the pastry is crisp and golden brown.

TOP TIP

Serve with fluffy mashed potato or chips for a hearty dinner.

Potatoes Dauphinoise

SERVES 6

PREPARATION TIME 20 MINUTES

COOKING TIME 1 HOUR 15–20 MINUTES

INGREDIENTS

400 ml / 14 fl. oz / 1 ¾ cups whole milk
350 ml / 12 fl. oz / 1 ½ cups double
    (heavy) cream
2 cloves of garlic, crushed
a few sprigs of thyme
1.25 kg / 2 lb 12 oz / 8 cups floury potatoes,
    peeled and sliced
2 tbsp butter, softened
salt and freshly ground black pepper
150 g / 5 oz / 1 ½ cups Gruyère, grated
a small handful of flat-leaf parsley,
    finely chopped

METHOD

- Preheat the oven to 190°C (170°C fan) /
  375F / gas 5.

- Warm the milk, cream, garlic and thyme
  in a saucepan until just simmering, then
  strain into a jug and set to one side.

- Cook the potato in a large saucepan of
  salted, boiling water for 6–8 minutes until
  starting to soften.

- Drain the potatoes and leave to cool
  slightly to one side.

- Butter an oval baking dish and pour in
  some of the milk and cream.

- Layer the potato on top and season with
  salt and pepper in between each layer.

- Pour over the rest of the milk and cream
  and cover with foil, then bake for 1 hour.

- Remove the foil after 1 hour and top with
  the Gruyère.

- Return the dish to the oven for
  15–20 minutes to brown on top.

- Remove from the oven and leave it to
  stand for 5 minutes.

- Garnish with chopped parsley
  before serving.

TOP TIP
You can use Comté or
Emmental cheese in
a pinch.

Mixed Roasted Roots

METHOD

- Put the parsnips, carrots and beetroot in a saucepan of salted water and bring to the boil.

- Simmer for 10 minutes, then drain well and leave to steam-dry for 2 minutes in the pan.

- Meanwhile, preheat the oven to 190°C (170°C fan) / 375F / gas 5.

- Tip the parsnips, carrots and beetroot into a baking dish and mix with the turnips, shallots, pepper, onion, garlic and thyme.

- Drizzle with olive oil and season well with salt and pepper, then roast for 45 minutes, stirring halfway through.

SERVES 4

PREPARATION TIME 15 MINUTES

COOKING TIME 45 MINUTES

INGREDIENTS

3 small parsnips, peeled and quartered
8 baby carrots, scrubbed
6 small beetroot, halved
8 baby turnips, scrubbed
8 small shallots
1 red pepper, cut into wedges
    2 small red onions, halved
1 bulb of garlic, halved horizontally
a few sprigs of thyme
4 tbsp olive oil
salt and black pepper

TOP TIP

These roasted vegetables are an easy accompaniment to any roast dinner.

Cheese Fondue

SERVES 6–8

PREPARATION TIME 30–35 MINUTES

COOKING TIME 25 MINUTES

INGREDIENTS

450 g / 1 lb / 3 cups baby new potatoes
1 clove of garlic, crushed
750 ml / 18 fl. oz / 3 cups dry white wine
2 tbsp cornflour (cornstarch)
225 g / 8 oz / 2 cups Comté, grated
225 g / 8 oz / 2 cups Emmental, grated
225 g / 8 oz / 2 cups Gruyère, grated
a couple of pinches of grated nutmeg
salt and freshly ground black pepper
gherkins in vinegar, drained
cocktail onions in vinegar, drained
1 crusty baguette, cut into 2 cm (1 in) cubes

METHOD

- Cook the potatoes in a large saucepan of salted, boiling water for 18–22 minutes until tender.
- Drain well and set to one side to cool.
- Rub the inside of a large, heavy-based saucepan with the crushed garlic clove.
- Combine the wine and cornflour in the saucepan and whisk thoroughly.
- Cook over a moderate heat until boiling, then reduce to a simmer.
- Whisk in the grated cheeses one by one. Stir continuously until the cheese is smooth and melted, then season with the nutmeg and seasoning.
- Continue to cook over a low heat for 12–15 minutes until the fondue has thickened.
- Transfer to a fondue pot and set over a portable flame to keep warm.
- Serve with the boiled potatoes, gherkins, onions and baguette cubes.

TOP TIP

Fondue is a sociable dish; why not try as a starter for your dinner party?

Broccoli and Halloumi Salad

SERVES 4

PREPARATION TIME 10 MINUTES

COOKING TIME 25 MINUTES

INGREDIENTS

175 g / 6 oz / 1 cup quinoa
2 tbsp olive oil
300 g / 10 ½ oz / 3 cups tenderstem
    broccoli, trimmed
salt and freshly ground black pepper
250 g / 9 oz / 1 ¾ cups halloumi slices
150 g / 5 oz / 1 ½ cups hazelnuts (cobnuts)
1 lemon, juiced

METHOD

- Preheat the grill to hot.
- Place a saucepan over a medium heat and add the quinoa.
- Cook the quinoa for 2–3 minutes until nutty in aroma. Cover with water and cook at a simmer for 12–14 minutes until tender.
- Drain well and rinse in cold water, then pat dry with kitchen paper.
- Heat the olive oil in a large sauté pan set over a medium heat until hot. Add the broccoli, salt and pepper and cover with a lid.
- Cook for 3–4 minutes until tender, then toss with the quinoa in a mixing bowl.
- Grill the halloumi for 2–3 minutes on both sides until golden and crisp. Drain on the kitchen paper, then grill the hazelnuts for a few minutes until lightly toasted.
- Toss the hazelnuts, halloumi and lemon juice with the quinoa and broccoli.
- Season with salt and pepper before serving.

TOP TIP
Substitute the hazelnuts (cobnuts) with walnuts.

Fig Salad

SERVES 4

PREPARATION TIME 10 MINUTES

COOKING TIME 5 MINUTES

INGREDIENTS

75 ml / 3 fl. oz / ⅓ cup extra-virgin olive oil
2 tbsp lemon juice
salt and freshly ground black pepper
225 g / 8 oz / 6 cups rocket (arugula), washed
1 large red onion, finely sliced
150 g / 5 oz / 1 ½ cups soft cheese
    (e.g. brie), cubed
8 fresh Bursa figs, cut into wedges

METHOD

- Whisk together the olive oil and lemon juice with a little salt and pepper in a large mixing bowl.
- Add the rocket leaves and red onion, tossing well to coat evenly.
- Add the cheese and half the figs, then toss again.
- Divide the salad between four serving plates and top with the remaining slices of fig.
- Serve immediately for best results.

TOP TIP
Add slices of avocado to make this salad more filling.

Black Forest Gateau

SERVES 8

PREPARATION TIME 30–35 MINUTES

COOKING TIME 35–40 MINUTES

INGREDIENTS

150 g / 5 oz / ⅔ cup margarine, softened
150 g / 5 oz / 1 cup self-raising flour, sifted
150 g / 5 oz / ⅔ cup caster (superfine) sugar
55 g / 2 oz / ⅓ cup cocoa powder, sifted
3 large eggs
2 tbsp kirsch
2 tbsp whole milk
500 ml / 18 fl. oz / 2 cups double
    (heavy) cream
65 g / 2 ½ oz / ½ cup icing (confectioners')
    sugar, sifted
1 tsp vanilla extract
600 g / 1 lb 5 oz / 3 cups canned cherries in
    syrup, drained
100 g / 3 ½ oz / ⅔ cup dark chocolate,
    roughly grated

METHOD

- Preheat the oven to 180°C (160°C fan) / 350F / gas 4 and grease and line a 23 cm (9 in) springform cake tin with greaseproof paper.

- Beat together the margarine, flour, sugar, cocoa powder, eggs and kirsch until smooth, then add the milk and beat briefly to incorporate.

- Spoon into the prepared cake tin and bake for 35–40 minutes until a cake tester comes out clean from the centre of the cake.

- Remove when ready and leave to cool on a wire rack before turning out from the tin.

- Whip the cream with the icing sugar and vanilla extract until it forms soft peaks.

- Spoon a third of the cream into a piping bag fitted with a star-shaped nozzle, and chill until needed.

- Horizontally slice the sponge into three even pieces. Lift one piece onto a cake stand.

- Top with a little cream, spread it out evenly and top with a third of the cherries.

- Position the second piece of cake on top and cover with more cream and half of the remaining cherries.

- Sit the final piece of cake on top and cover the top and sides of the cake with an even layer of cream.

- Press grated chocolate into the cream on the sides of the cake, spooning the remainder on top of the centre of the cake.

- Pipe swirls of cream around the edge of the cake top, then place a cherry on top of each swirl.

- Cover and chill the gateau if not serving straight away.

Baked Alaska

SERVES 6–8

PREPARATION TIME 20–25 MINUTES

COOKING TIME 25–30 MINUTES

INGREDIENTS

1 tbsp sunflower oil

225 g / 8 oz / 1 cup caster (superfine) sugar

110 g / 4 oz / ½ cup margarine, softened

110 g / 4 oz / ⅔ cup self-raising flour, sifted

2 tbsp cocoa powder, sifted

2 medium eggs

900 g / 2 lb / 4 cups vanilla ice cream,
    softened

2 large egg whites

a pinch of salt

a pinch of cream of tartar

METHOD

- Preheat the oven to 180°C (160°C fan) /
  350F / gas 4.

- Brush the inside of a 900 g / 2 lb pudding
  basin with oil and line with cling film.
  Grease and line an 18 cm (7 in) cake tin
  with greaseproof paper.

- Beat together half of the sugar with the
  margarine, flour, cocoa powder and eggs
  in a large mixing bowl for 2–3 minutes
  until smooth.

- Spoon the batter into the prepared
  cake tin and settle evenly, then bake for
  20–25 minutes until risen and a cake tester
  comes out clean from the centre. Remove
  to a wire rack to cool.

- Fill the prepared pudding basin with
  the softened ice cream, stopping about
  4 cm (1 ½ in) from the rim. Turn out the
  sponge from the tin and sit it on top of the
  ice cream, trimming it to fit if necessary.

- Cover the basin with a large sheet of cling
  film and freeze it while you prepare
  the meringue.

- Beat the egg whites with a pinch of salt
  until softly peaked, then add half of the
  remaining sugar and continue to beat
  until glossy. Add the cream of tartar and
  the rest of the sugar, beating for another
  3 minutes until thick and stiff.

- Increase the oven to 240°C (220°C fan) /
  475F / gas 9.

- Remove the pudding basin from the
  freezer and turn out the ice cream and
  cake onto a trivet sat on top of a baking
  tray. Spread the meringue evenly over it
  with a spatula until completely covered.

- Bake for 3–4 minutes or until the
  meringue starts to brown, then serve.

Festive Fruit Salad

SERVES 4

PREPARATION TIME 15 MINUTES

INGREDIENTS

2 pomegranates
4 large oranges, peeled and segmented
2 pink grapefruits, peeled and segmented
300 g / 10 ½ oz / 2 cups seedless white
    grapes, halved
150 ml / 5 fl. oz / ⅔ cup clear apple juice
a few drops of vanilla extract

METHOD

- Cut the pomegranates in half and extract the seeds by firmly tapping the skin side of the pomegranate halves with a wooden spoon.
- Collect the seeds in a large bowl, then remove half to another bowl.
- Add the orange and grapefruit segments and the grapes to one of the bowls.
- Whisk together the apple juice and vanilla extract, then add to the bowl with all of the fruit.
- Divide the fruit between serving bowls and top with the remaining pomegranate seeds.

TOP TIP
Serve with double (heavy) cream or sorbet for an indulgent dessert.

Apple Snow

METHOD

- Preheat the oven to 200°C (180°C fan) / 400F / gas 6.
- Put the apples, sugar and cinnamon in a saucepan with 4 tbsp of cold water. Put a lid on the pan then cook over a gentle heat for 10 minutes, stirring occasionally. Taste the apple and stir in a little more sugar if it is too sharp.
- Whisk the egg whites until stiff, then gradually add the sugar and whisk until the mixture is thick and shiny.
- Spoon half of the apple compote into 6 ovenproof dessert glasses. Fold half of the meringue into the rest of the compote and spoon it on top, then add a final layer of meringue.
- Transfer the glasses to the oven and bake for 10 minutes or until the tops are golden brown.

SERVES 6

PREPARATION TIME 15 MINUTES

COOKING TIME 20 MINUTES

INGREDIENTS

2 large cooking apples, peeled and diced
3 tbsp light brown sugar
½ tsp ground cinnamon
FOR THE MERINGUE
4 large egg whites
110 g / 4 oz / ½ cup caster (superfine) sugar

TOP TIP

Cooking apples are quite tart, so add a bit more sugar if necesssary.

Christmas Day

Gravadlax

METHOD

- Juice the lemons into a large mixing bowl. Add the smoked salmon slices and stir well to coat in the juice. Cover and chill.

- Blanch the chives in a large saucepan of boiling water for 10 seconds.

- Drain well and pat dry.

- Shape the smoked salmon slices into purses, tying their tops with the blanched chives.

- Serve in platters, garnished with grapefruit.

SERVES 8

PREPARATION TIME 10 MINUTES

COOKING TIME 1 MINUTE

INGREDIENTS

2 lemons
450 g / 1 lb / 3 cups smoked salmon slices
a large bunch of chives
1 white grapefruit, peeled, segmented and diced

TOP TIP
Add a small dollop of cream cheese on the side for a different taste.

Baked Camembert

SERVES 8

PREPARATION TIME 10 MINUTES

COOKING TIME 15 MINUTES

INGREDIENTS

2 wheels of Camembert, in their boxes
2 cloves of garlic, crushed
flaked sea salt

METHOD

- Preheat the oven to 200°C (180°C fan) / 400F / gas 6.
- Remove any wrapping from the Camemberts and replace them back in their boxes.
- Rub their tops with crushed garlic and season with sea salt.
- Place the Camembert on a baking tray and bake for 15 minutes until the inside of the cheeses are melted.
- Remove from the oven and pierce the skin before serving.

TOP TIP

Serve with crusty bread to dip, and red onion chutney for added sweetness.

Traditional Roast Turkey

SERVES 8
PREPARATION TIME 25 MINUTES
COOKING TIME 3 HOURS 20 MINUTES

INGREDIENTS

4 oranges, peeled, segmented and diced
4 medium onions, chopped
a few sprigs of rosemary, chopped
a few sprigs of oregano
salt and freshly ground black pepper
3 kg / 6 lb 10 oz turkey, cleaned and trimmed
110 g / 4 oz / ½ cup clarified butter
750 g / 1 lb 10 oz / 5 cups waxy potatoes, halved
450 g / 1 lb oz / 3 cups baby carrots
450 g / 1 lb oz / 3 cups Brussels sprouts,
    scored on their undersides
2 tbsp olive oil
1 tbsp honey

METHOD

- Preheat the oven to 180°C (160°C fan) / 350F / gas 4.
- Combine the oranges and onions with the herbs and seasoning in a large mixing bowl.
- Season the turkey inside and out with salt and pepper, then fill with the stuffing.
- Tie with kitchen string and place in a roasting tray, smearing it with half of the clarified butter. Season with salt and pepper.
- Roast on the bottom shelf of the oven for 2 hours, basting occasionally with the remaining clarified butter.
- After 2 hours, place the potatoes around the turkey and roast for a further 45 minutes until the thickest part of the thigh registers at least 71°C / 160F on a meat thermometer.
- Remove the turkey from the oven and cover it loosely with kitchen foil, leaving it to rest for at least 30 minutes. Return the potatoes to the oven to crisp.
- Meanwhile, cook the carrots and sprouts in separate large saucepans of salted, boiling water for 15–18 minutes until tender.
- Drain well and toss the carrots immediately with the olive oil and honey. Drain the sprouts when tender.
- Season the vegetables with salt and pepper and serve alongside the turkey, potatoes and sprouts.

TOP TIP
Cranberry sauce is a classic accompaniment to a traditional turkey roast.

Stuffed Turkey Breast

SERVES 6

PREPARATION TIME 20 MINUTES

COOKING TIME 40 MINUTES

INGREDIENTS

250 g / 9 oz / 1 ¼ cups cooked chestnuts
1 large egg
30 g / 1 oz / ⅓ cup fresh white breadcrumbs
50 ml / 1 ¾ oz / ¼ cup milk
2 shallots, finely chopped
900 g / 2 lb / 4 ½ cups turkey breast
50 g / 1 ¾ oz / ¼ cup butter, softened
salt and black pepper

METHOD

- Reserve five chestnuts and put the rest in a food processor with the egg, breadcrumbs, milk and shallots. Blend to a fine purée.

- Roughly chop the reserved chestnuts and stir them into the stuffing, then season well with salt and pepper.

- Cut the turkey breast almost in half horizontally without cutting all the way through, then open it out like a book. Spoon the stuffing in a line down the centre, then fold the turkey back over and tie securely with string.

- Preheat the oven to 220°C (200°C fan) / 430F / gas 7. Lay the turkey in a greaseproof paper-lined roasting tin and smear with butter.

- Season with salt and pepper, then roast for 40 minutes or until the turkey is cooked all the way through. Carve into slices to serve.

TOP TIP

Distribute the stuffing evenly to ensure a neat cross-section when serving.

Roast Goose with Figs

SERVES 8

PREPARATION TIME 40 MINUTES

COOKING TIME 2 HOURS 45–50 MINUTES

INGREDIENTS

2.5 kg / 5 lb 10 oz goose, cleaned and trimmed
    of excess fat
4 Bursa figs, halved
55 g / 2 oz / ¼ cup unsalted butter, softened
2 tbsp honey
salt and freshly ground black pepper
a few sprigs of flat-leaf parsley, to garnish

METHOD

- Preheat the oven to 220°C (200°C fan) / 425F / gas 7.

- Sit the goose in a large roasting tray and season its insides with salt and pepper.

- Stuff the cavity with a few fig halves and smear the skin with butter. Drizzle with honey and season with salt and pepper.

- Arrange the remaining fig halves in and around the goose in the tray.

- Roast for 30 minutes, then reduce the oven to 180°C (160°C fan) / 350°F / gas 4. Roast for a further 2 hours 10–20 minutes or until the thickest part of the thigh registers at least 71°C / 160F on a meat thermometer.

- Remove the goose from the oven and cover loosely with kitchen foil, leaving it to rest for at least 30 minutes.

- Serve with a garnish of parsley.

TOP TIP
If you don't have a large baking tray, look out for good-quality disposable ones.

Roast Partridge

SERVES 2

PREPARATION TIME 15 MINUTES

COOKING TIME 15 MINUTES

INGREDIENTS

2 tbsp olive oil
2 partridge, halved
2 tbsp butter
75 g / 2 ½ oz / 1 cup chanterelles, cleaned
1 clove of garlic, crushed
1 tbsp parsley leaves
Freshly cooked pappardelle to serve
Salt and black pepper

METHOD

- Preheat the oven to 200°C (180°C fan) / 400F / gas 6.

- Heat the oil in an oven-proof frying pan and season the partridge all over with salt and pepper. Fry the partridge skin side down until golden brown, then turn them over and transfer the pan to the oven.

- Roast the partridge for 5 minutes, then transfer to a warm plate and leave to rest for 10 minutes.

- Meanwhile, add the butter to the partridge pan and sauté the chanterelles for 5 minutes. Stir in the garlic and cook for 1 minute, then toss with the pappardelle and parsley. Serve with the partridge.

TOP TIP
Use chestnut mushrooms if you cannot find chanterelles.

Roast Duck Stuffed with Dried Fruit

SERVES 2

PREPARATION TIME 20 MINUTES

COOKING TIME 1 HOUR

INGREDIENTS

2 large duck breasts
75 g / 2 ½ oz / ⅓ cup dried apricots
75 g / 2 ½ oz / ⅓ cup dried prunes, pitted
75 g / 2 ½ oz / ⅓ cup dried pears
450 g / 1 lb / 1 cup potatoes, peeled
    and cubed
2 tbsp rosemary leaves
salt and black pepper

METHOD

- Preheat the oven to 200°C (180°C fan) / 400F / gas 6.
- Lay one duck breast skin side down on a chopping board and top with the dried fruits. Lay the other duck breast on top, skin side up, then tie securely with string along its length.
- Put the potatoes in a baking dish, then sprinkle with rosemary and season with salt and pepper. Lay the duck joint on top, then transfer the dish to the oven and roast for 1 hour, turning the duck and stirring the potatoes half way through.
- Carve the duck into thick slices and serve with the potatoes.

TOP TIP
Garnish with sprigs of fresh rosemary for an aromatic scent.

Nut Roast with Cranberries

SERVES 6

PREPARATION TIME 30 MINUTES

COOKING TIME 35–40 MINUTES

INGREDIENTS

225 g / 8 oz / 2 cups cashews

225 g / 8 oz / 2 cups hazelnuts (cobnuts)

125 g / 4 ½ oz / 1 cup cooked
    chestnuts, chopped

55 ml / 2 fl. oz / ¼ cup sunflower oil

2 small onions, finely chopped

2 stalks of celery, finely chopped

salt and freshly ground black pepper

2 cloves of garlic, minced

100 g / 3 ½ oz / 1 cup fresh breadcrumbs

100 g / 3 ½ oz / 1 cup cranberries

a small handful of sage leaves, chopped

a few sprigs of thyme, chopped

a few sprigs of flat-leaf parsley, chopped

1 lemon, juiced

2 medium eggs, beaten

2 tbsp olive oil

200 g / 7 oz / 4 cups baby spinach, washed

225 g / 8 oz / 2 cups goats' cheese

METHOD

- Preheat the oven to 180°C (160°C fan) / 350F / gas 4 and grease a 450 g / 1 lb loaf tin.

- Toast the nuts in a dry frying pan set over a medium heat until hot, then tip them into a food processor and pulse until coarsely chopped.

- Heat the sunflower oil in the frying pan and sweat the onion, celery and a little salt over a medium heat until softened.

- Add the garlic and cook for a further minute, then stir in the breadcrumbs and remove the pan from the heat.

- Put the onion mixture into a large bowl and add the nuts, cranberries and herbs, reserving a few sage leaves as a garnish. Season with salt and pepper, then stir in the lemon juice and the eggs.

- Heat the olive oil in a large sauté pan and cook the spinach with a little seasoning until just wilted.

- Tip the wilted spinach into a colander and press it against the sides to extract the excess water.

- Spoon half the nut mixture into the loaf tin, pressing it down with the back of a spoon. Top with the goats' cheese then the spinach, following it with the remaining nut mixture.

- Pack the mixture down firmly and bake the nut roast for 35–40 minutes.

- Remove from the oven and let the loaf cool a little in the tin before turning out, slicing and serving.

Vegetable Wellington

SERVES 6–8

PREPARATION TIME 25–30 MINUTES

COOKING TIME 22–25 MINUTES

INGREDIENTS

75 ml / 3 fl. oz / ⅓ cup olive oil
2 courgettes (zucchinis), sliced
salt and freshly ground black pepper
1 aubergine (eggplant), sliced
1 large red pepper, sliced
1 large yellow pepper, sliced
1 large red onion, sliced
200 g / 7 oz / 4 cups baby spinach, washed
300 g / 10 ½ oz ready-made puff pastry
a little plain (all-purpose) flour, for dusting
300 g / 10 ½ oz / 2 cups halloumi, sliced
1 small egg, beaten

METHOD

- Preheat the oven to 200°C (180°C fan) / 400F / gas 6.

- Heat a little olive oil in a large sauté pan set over a moderate heat and add the courgette slices and a little seasoning. Sauté for 4–5 minutes until softened and starting to brown.

- Remove from the pan, then add a little more oil, the aubergine and a little seasoning. Sauté for 3–4 minutes until softened and starting to brown.

- Remove from the pan, then add a little more olive oil, the peppers, onion and seasoning. Sauté for 3–4 minutes until softened, then remove from the pan.

- Add the remaining oil, baby spinach and seasoning and sauté for 2–3 minutes until wilted.

- Remove from the pan and place in a colander to drain.

- Roll out the pastry on a lightly floured surface, into a rectangle approximately 45 cm x 35 cm x 1 cm (18 in x 14 in x ½ in).

- Brush the perimeter with a little beaten egg, then layer the vegetables, cheese and spinach in the centre of the pastry, seasoning between the layers.

- Bring the pastry edges up and over the vegetable filling, sealing on top to enclose the filling.

- Brush the unbaked Wellington with beaten egg and place on a baking tray.

- Bake for 22–25 minutes until golden and puffed.

- Remove from the oven and leave to stand briefly before slicing and serving.

Roast Potatoes with Garlic and Rosemary

SERVES 6–8

PREPARATION TIME 30–35 MINUTES

COOKING TIME 45–50 MINUTES

INGREDIENTS

1.25 kg / 2 lb 12 oz / 8 cups floury potatoes,
   peeled and cut into chunks
150 g / 5 oz / ²/₃ cup goose or duck fat
1 head of garlic, smashed with
   cloves separated
a few sprigs of rosemary
salt and freshly ground black pepper

METHOD

- Preheat the oven to 220°C (200°C fan) / 425F / gas 7.
- Place the potatoes in a large saucepan and cover with water.
- Cook over a moderate heat until boiling, then continue to cook for 15–18 minutes until tender to the point of a knife.
- Drain and cover with a tea towel.
- Place the fat in a large roasting tray and let it warm in the oven for 10 minutes.
- Carefully remove after 10 minutes and add the potatoes to the hot fat, tossing with a pair of tongs to coat evenly.
- Add the garlic cloves and rosemary, tossing well again.
- Return to the oven for 45–50 minutes until golden and crisp on the outside.
- Season with salt and pepper before serving.

TOP TIP

For vegetarian potatoes, use olive oil in place of the fat.

Pigs in Blankets

METHOD

- Preheat the oven to 200°C (180°C fan) / 400F / gas 6.

- Wrap the chipolatas with pieces of bacon and arrange them on a baking tray, making sure they're spaced apart.

- Mix together the sausage meat, onion, sage and seasoning until thoroughly combined.

- Shape into rough balls and arrange alongside the wrapped chipolatas.

- Roast in the oven for 18–22 minutes until the chipolatas are cooked through and the sausage balls are browned all over.

- Remove from the oven and arrange in a serving bowl, garnished with bay leaves and a little black pepper.

SERVES 8

PREPARATION TIME 10 MINUTES

COOKING TIME 18–22 MINUTES

INGREDIENTS

16 chipolata sausages
8 rashers of bacon, cut in half
450 g / 1 lb / 3 cups sausage meat
½ onion, finely chopped
½ tsp dried sage
a small handful of bay leaves
salt and freshly ground black pepper

TOP TIP

Any leftovers can be reheated on Boxing Day in a microwave.

Braised Red Cabbage

METHOD

- Combine the cabbage, red wine vinegar, water, sugar, cinnamon stick and seasoning in a heavy-based saucepan.
- Cover with a lid and braise over a low heat for 1 hour until the cabbage has softened.
- Add the cranberries and continue to braise, covered, for 20 minutes until they are soft and juicy.
- Adjust the seasoning to taste and spoon into bowls.
- Garnish with bay leaves and thyme leaves before serving.

SERVES 6–8

PREPARATION TIME 10–15 MINUTES

COOKING TIME 1 HOUR 20 MINUTES

INGREDIENTS

2 small red cabbages, shredded
125 ml / 4 ½ fl. oz / ½ cup red wine vinegar
55 ml / 2 fl. oz / ¼ cup water
55 g / 2 oz / ¼ cup caster (superfine) sugar
5 cm (2 in) piece of cinnamon stick
salt and freshly ground black pepper
125 g / 4 ½ oz / 1 cup cranberries
a few bay leaves
a few sprigs of thyme, leaves stripped

TOP TIP
This dish can be served cold, too. Keep it in the fridge until you use it.

Glazed Carrots and Parsnips

SERVES 6–8

PREPARATION TIME 20 MINUTES

COOKING TIME 30–35 MINUTES

INGREDIENTS

600 g / 1 lb 5 oz / 4 cups carrots, peeled and cut into batons

600 g / 1 lb 5 oz / 4 cups parsnips, peeled and cut into batons

75 ml / 3 fl. oz / ⅓ cup honey, warmed

2 tbsp coriander seeds, lightly crushed

salt and freshly ground black pepper

METHOD

- Preheat the oven to 190°C (170°C fan) / 375F / gas 5.
- Place the carrots and parsnips in a large saucepan of salted water.
- Heat over a moderate heat until boiling. Reduce to a simmer for 10 minutes until just tender to the point of a knife.
- Drain well and leave to steam dry for a few minutes.
- Toss with the honey, coriander seeds and seasoning.
- Arrange in a large roasting tray and roast for 30–35 minutes until glazed and lightly browned.
- Remove from the oven and leave to stand briefly before serving.

TOP TIP

Carrots can be left unpeeled, as long as they are cleaned thoroughly.

Brussels Sprouts with Pancetta

SERVES 8

PREPARATION TIME 15 MINUTES

COOKING TIME 25–35 MINUTES

INGREDIENTS

- 900 g / 2 lb / 6 cups Brussels sprouts, scored on their undersides
- 2 tbsp unsalted butter
- 1 tbsp sunflower oil
- 2 red onions, sliced
- 150 g / 5 oz / 1 cup pancetta lardons
- salt and freshly ground black pepper

METHOD

- Cook the sprouts in a large saucepan of salted, boiling water for 18–22 minutes until tender.
- Drain the sprouts and keep warm to one side.
- Melt the butter with the oil in a large sauté or saucepan set over a medium heat until hot.
- Add the onion and sauté for 5–6 minutes until softened, stirring occasionally.
- Add the pancetta and a little salt and pepper, stirring well.
- Increase the heat a little and sauté until the pancetta is golden and crisp at the edges.
- Spoon the sprouts into a serving dish and top with the pancetta and onions before serving.

TOP TIP

Smoked bacon lardons can be in used instead of the pancetta.

Yorkshire Puddings

SERVES 4

PREPARATION TIME 5 MINUTES

COOKING TIME 25 MINUTES

INGREDIENTS

4 tsp beef dripping
75 g / 2 ½ oz / ½ cup plain (all-purpose) flour
2 large eggs
100 ml / 3 ½ oz / ½ cup whole milk

METHOD

- Preheat the oven to 230°C (210°C fan) / 450F / gas 8.
- Put 1 tsp of dripping into each hole of a 4-hole Yorkshire pudding tin, then put it in the oven to heat.
- Put the flour in a large jug with a pinch of salt and make a well in the centre. Break in the eggs and pour in the milk then use a whisk to gradually incorporate all of the flour from round the outside.
- Carefully take the tin out of the oven and immediately divide the batter between the holes. Return the tin to the oven and bake for 25 minutes without opening the oven door.
- Serve straight away.

TOP TIP
Leave the batter to stand in the fridge for 30 minutes before cooking.

Stuffing Balls

SERVES 6

PREPARATION TIME 15 MINUTES

COOKING TIME 25 MINUTES

INGREDIENTS

2 tbsp olive oil

1 onion, finely chopped

2 cloves of garlic, crushed

2 tbsp sage leaves, finely chopped

450 g / 1 lb / 3 cups pork sausage meat

100 g / 3 ½ oz / 1 ⅓ cups fresh white
    breadcrumbs

100 g / 3 ½ oz / ½ cup dried
    apricots, chopped

50 g / 1 ¾ oz / ½ cup walnuts, chopped

METHOD

- Preheat the oven to 200°C (180°C fan) / 390F / gas 6 and oil a roasting tin.

- Heat the oil in a large sauté pan and fry the onion, garlic and sage together for 5 minutes or until softened.

- Scrape the mixture into a mixing bowl and leave to cool to room temperature.

- Add the sausage meat, breadcrumbs, apricots and walnuts to the mixing bowl and season with salt and pepper, then knead it all together with your hands until it is well mixed.

- Roll the stuffing into clementine-sized balls and space them out in the roasting tin. Roast the stuffing balls for 25 minutes or until cooked all the way through and nicely browned on top.

TOP TIP
Substitute the apricots for the same amount of apple, cut into cubes.

Christmas Pudding

SERVES 6–8

PREPARATION TIME 30 MINUTES

COOKING TIME 6 HOURS

INGREDIENTS

150 g / 5 oz / ⅔ cup shredded suet
110 g / 4 oz / 1 cup white breadcrumbs
75 g / 3 oz / ½ cup self-raising flour, sifted
225 g / 8 oz / 1 ⅓ cups soft dark brown sugar
1 tsp ground allspice
1 tsp ground nutmeg
110 g / 4 oz / ⅔ cup raisins
110 g / 4 oz / ⅔ cup sultanas
300 g / 10 ½ oz / 2 cups currants
2 tbsp chopped mixed peel
2 tbsp ground almonds
1 medium Bramley apple, peeled,
    cored and finely diced
1 lemon, zested
1 orange, zested
75 ml / 3 fl. oz / ⅓ cup dark rum
110 ml / 4 fl. oz / ½ cup stout
2 large eggs
2 tbsp unsalted butter, softened

METHOD

- Place the suet, breadcrumbs, flour, sugar and ground spices in a large mixing bowl. Stir well with a spoon to combine evenly.

- Add the dried fruit, mixed peel and ground almonds and stir again, then add the apple and citrus zests, giving the mixture another good stir.

- In a separate mixing bowl, combine the rum, stout and eggs, whisking well to combine. Add to the main mixing bowl with all the other ingredients and stir really well until you have a sloppy mixture. Cover the bowl and leave the mixture to soak overnight.

- When you are ready to steam the pudding, lightly grease a 900 g / 2 lb pudding bowl with the butter. Pack the mixture into it, pressing down really well to make sure it all fits into the pudding bowl.

- Cover the top of the pudding batter with a double layer of greaseproof paper and cover the base of the bowl with a layer of kitchen foil.

- Tie the foil against the rim of the pudding bowl with kitchen string to secure the foil, then make an additional handle from string and attach it to the string tied around the rim of the pudding bowl.

- Place the pudding bowl in a steamer set over a saucepan of gently simmering water. Steam the pudding for 6 hours, making sure you top up the water in the saucepan when it starts to run dry.

- Remove after 6 hours steaming and let it cool to one side. Once cool enough to handle, remove the foil and greaseproof paper.

- Run a palette knife around the inside of the pudding basin to loosen the pudding. Invert it onto a plate and serve warm with brandy butter or ice cream.

Almond and Butterscotch Semifreddo

SERVES 6

PREPARATION TIME 1 HOUR

COOKING TIME 5 MINUTES

FREEZING TIME 6 HOURS

INGREDIENTS

2 large eggs, separated
100 g / 3 ½ oz / 1 cup icing
    (confectioners') sugar
600 ml / 1 pint / 2 ½ cups double
    (heavy) cream
3 tbsp amaretto liqueur
50 g / 1 ¾ oz / ½ cup flaked
    (slivered) almonds

FOR THE BUTTERSCOTCH SAUCE

85 g / 3 oz / ½ cup butter
85 ml / 3 fl. oz / ⅓ cup double (heavy) cream
85 g / 3 oz / ¼ cup golden syrup
85 g / 3 oz / ½ cup dark brown sugar

METHOD

- Whisk the egg whites in a very clean bowl until stiff, then whisk in half of the icing sugar.

- Whisk the egg yolks with the rest of the icing sugar in a separate bowl for 4 minutes or until very thick.

- Whip the cream with the amaretto in a third bowl until it holds its shape. Fold the egg yolk mixture into the cream, then fold in the egg whites.

- Line a small loaf tin with cling film, then pour in the cream mixture and level the top. Freeze for 6 hours or preferably overnight.

- To make the butterscotch sauce, stir the butter, cream, syrup and sugar together over a low heat until the butter melts and the sugar dissolves. Increase the heat and simmer for 2 minutes or until thick and homogenised. Leave to cool to room temperature.

- Remove the semifreddo from the freezer 45 minutes before serving. Unmould it onto a serving plate and scatter over the almonds, then drizzle with the butterscotch sauce. Cut into 6 wedges and serve immediately.

TOP TIP

Replace the flaked almonds with chopped hazelnuts (cobnuts) for variation.

Sticky Toffee Pudding

METHOD

- Preheat the oven to 180°C (160°C fan) / 350F / gas 4 and grease and line a 23 cm (8 in) springform cake tin with greaseproof paper.
- Combine the dates, water and bicarbonate of soda in a saucepan. Warm the mixture over a medium heat until it approaches boiling point, then remove from the heat and set to one side.
- Place the flour in a large mixing bowl and cream together 175 g / 6 oz / ¾ cup of the sugar with 110 g / 4 oz / ½ cup of the butter in a separate bowl until pale.
- Beat in the eggs, one by one, then beat in the vanilla extract and baking powder. Fold through the flour in thirds, followed by the date mixture.
- Spoon into the prepared tin and bake in the oven for 40–50 minutes until risen and a cake tester comes out almost clean from the centre.
- Remove the pudding from the oven and leave it to cool slightly on a wire rack.
- Warm together the cream and golden syrup with the remaining sugar and butter in a saucepan set over a medium heat
- Stir occasionally until the sugar has dissolved and the sauce thickens.
- Skewer holes all over the cake and pour half of the sauce over it, leaving it to sink in.
- Leave the pudding to stand for 5 minutes before turning out and serving with more sauce on top.

SERVES 6–8
PREPARATION TIME 25 MINUTES
COOKING TIME 40–50 MINUTES

INGREDIENTS

200 g / 7 oz / 1 ¼ cups pitted dates
110 ml / 4 fl. oz / ½ cup water
½ tsp bicarbonate of (baking) soda
225 g / 8 oz / 1 ½ cups plain (all-purpose) flour, sifted
300 g / 10 ½ oz / 1 ¾ cups soft brown sugar
225 g / 8 oz / 1 cup unsalted butter, softened
2 large eggs
1 tsp vanilla extract
1 tsp baking powder
150 ml / 5 fl. oz / ⅔ cup double (heavy) cream
2 tbsp golden syrup

Boxing Day

Butternut Squash Soup

SERVES 4

PREPARATION TIME 20 MINUTES

COOKING TIME 30–35 MINUTES

INGREDIENTS

55 ml / 2 fl. oz / ¼ cup sunflower oil

1 large onion, chopped

2 cloves of garlic, chopped

2 tsp mild curry powder

1 tsp ground cumin

1 medium carrot, peeled and diced

1 kg / 2 lb 4 oz butternut squash, peeled, deseeded and diced

1 l / 1 pint 16 fl. oz / 4 cups vegetable stock, hot

100 g / 3 ½ oz / ½ cup crème fraiche

a few thyme leaves

4 crusty brown rolls, to serve

salt and freshly ground black pepper

METHOD

- Heat the oil in a large pan and gently cook the onion with a little salt until soft but not brown.

- Add the garlic and cook for 1 minute, then stir in the ground spices and cook for 2 minutes.

- Add the carrot and butternut squash, stirring well to coat the vegetables in the oil, then add the stock.

- Once the soup is simmering, cook gently for 20–25 minutes or until the carrot and squash are very tender.

- Purée the soup in a food processor or with a stick blender.

- Reheat gently and season to taste with salt and pepper.

- Ladle into bowls, garnish with crème fraiche, thyme leaves and a little more black pepper.

- Serve with crusty brown rolls on the side.

TOP TIP

Try to keep the butternut squash pieces an even size for consistent cooking.

Turkey Sandwiches

SERVES 4

PREPARATION TIME 10 MINUTES

COOKING TIME 10 MINUTES

INGREDIENTS

8 rashers of streaky bacon
8 slices of multigrain bread
55 g / 2 oz / ¼ cup butter, softened
450 g / 1 lb / 3 cups leftover roast turkey, cold
200 g / 7 oz / 1 cup cranberry sauce
a large handful of celery tops, to garnish
salt and freshly ground black pepper

METHOD

- Preheat the grill to a high setting.
- Arrange the bacon on a grilling tray and grill for 3–4 minutes, turning once, until golden and crisp.
- Remove and drain on kitchen paper.
- Toast the bread under the grill or in a toaster, flipping once to toast both sides.
- Spread half of the toast slices with butter then top with slices of turkey and bacon.
- Top with cranberry sauce and celery tops, season to taste, then place the other slices of toast on top.
- Serve immediately for best results.

TOP TIP

Add a cheese of your preference for a naughty-but-nice addition!

Turkey Curry

METHOD

- Blitz the chopped turkey in a food processor until minced.

- Heat 3 tbsp of the oil in a large saucepan set over a medium heat and cook the onion and garlic until lightly browned.

- Mix together the remaining oil, tomato purée, spices and ¼ tsp salt to form a thick paste.

- Stir the paste into the onion mixture and cook for 30 seconds, stirring frequently.

- Stir in the minced turkey and cook for 2 minutes.

- Add the coconut milk and simmer for 8–10 minutes until piping hot. If the mixture is too thick, add a little hot water to thin it out.

- Stir in the ginger and lemon juice and season to taste.

- Serve the curry over basmati rice and garnish with coriander on top.

SERVES 4

PREPARATION TIME 10 MINUTES

COOKING TIME 15–20 MINUTES

INGREDIENTS

450 g / 1 lb / 3 cups cooked turkey, chopped
55 ml / 2 fl. oz / ¼ cup sunflower oil
1 large onion, finely chopped
4 cloves of garlic, minced
1 tbsp tomato purée
2 tsp ground cumin
1 tsp ground coriander
1 tsp turmeric
¼ tsp chilli (chili) powder
¼ tsp garam masala
salt and freshly ground black pepper
400 ml / 14 fl. oz / 2 cups coconut milk
1 tsp grated ginger
1 tbsp lemon juice
cooked basmati rice, to serve
a few sprigs of coriander (cilantro), to garnish

TOP TIP
You can use leftover chicken instead of turkey; follow the same cooking steps.

Turkey and Ham Pie

SERVES 4–6

PREPARATION TIME 25–30 MINUTES

COOKING TIME 20–25 MINUTES

INGREDIENTS

2 tbsp unsalted butter

250 g / 9 oz / 2 cups cooked Brussels
sprouts, chopped

salt and freshly ground black pepper

400 g / 14 oz / 2 ⅔ cups cooked turkey, diced

300 g / 10 ½ oz / 2 cups cooked
gammon, diced

350 ml / 12 fl. oz / 1 ½ cups leftover gravy

110 ml / 4 fl. oz / ½ cup water

250 g / 9 oz ready-made puff pastry

a little plain (all-purpose) flour, for dusting

1 small egg, beaten

METHOD

- Preheat the oven to 200°C (180°C fan) /
  400F / gas 6.

- Melt the butter in a large saucepan set over
  a medium heat until hot.

- Add the sprouts and seasoning, sautéing
  for 2–3 minutes and stirring frequently.

- Add the cooked turkey and gammon and
  stir well. Continue to cook for 2–3 minutes,
  then cover with the gravy and water.

- Cook for 5–6 minutes until simmering,
  then season to taste and set to one side.

- Divide the pastry in half and roll out on a
  lightly floured surface into rounds
  approximately 1 cm (½ in) thick.

- Fill two 450 g / 1 lb pudding bowls with
  the turkey filling and top with the rounds
  of pastry, sealing them against the rims of
  the bowls.

- Trim any excess pastry and bore a small
  hole in their tops to allow steam to escape.

- Brush with the beaten egg and arrange on
  a large baking tray.

- Bake for 20–25 minutes until the pastry is
  golden and puffed, then remove from the
  oven and leave to stand for 5 minutes
  before serving.

TOP TIP
Experiment with leftover
meats and vegetables;
carrots would work
well in this dish.

Bubble and Squeak

METHOD

- Melt the butter with the oil in a large sauté pan set over a moderate heat until hot.

- Add the chopped cabbage or sprouts and some seasoning, then sauté for 2–3 minutes.

- Add the crushed potatoes and continue to cook for 5–6 minutes until piping hot.

- Season to taste and serve straight from the pan.

SERVES 6–8

PREPARATION TIME 10 MINUTES

COOKING TIME 7–9 MINUTES

INGREDIENTS

2 tbsp unsalted butter

1 tbsp sunflower oil

300 g / 10 ½ oz / 3 cups leftover cooked cabbage or Brussels sprouts, chopped

salt and freshly ground black pepper

600 g / 1 lb / 5 oz / 4 cups leftover roast potatoes, crushed

TOP TIP

Add a poached or fried egg on top for a more substantial dish.

Chicken, Tomato and Mushroom Stew

SERVES 4

PREPARATION TIME 5 MINUTES

COOKING TIME 30 MINUTES

INGREDIENTS

2 tbsp olive oil
4 skinless chicken breasts, halved
1 onion, chopped
1 carrot, chopped
1 celery stick, chopped
2 cloves of garlic, crushed
400 g / 14 oz / 2 cups canned tomatoes, chopped
200 ml / 7 fl. oz / ¾ cup chicken stock
150 g / 5 ½ oz / 2 cups button mushrooms
mashed potato to serve
2 tbsp flat leaf parsley, finely chopped
salt and freshly ground black pepper

METHOD

- Heat the oil in a wide saucepan and sear the chicken all over. Remove to a plate with a slotted spoon.
- Add the onion, carrot, celery and garlic to the pan and cook without browning for 5 minutes. Pour in the tomatoes and stock and bring to the boil, then return the chicken to the pan and simmer gently for 10 minutes.
- Add the mushrooms to the pan and simmer for another 10 minutes, then season to taste with salt and pepper.
- Serve the stew with mashed potato and the parsley sprinkled over.

TOP TIP
Serve with rice or a simple green salad.

Prosciutto-wrapped Sausage Sandwiches

SERVES 2

PREPARATION TIME 5 MINUTES

COOKING TIME 15 MINUTES

INGREDIENTS

4 pork and herb sausages

4 slices prosciutto

2 tbsp olive oil

2 bread rolls, halved

a handful of rocket (arugula) leaves

4 generous sprigs of sage (leaves separated)

METHOD

- Wrap the sausages with the prosciutto, then fry them in the oil over a low heat for 15 minutes, turning occasionally.

- Add the sage leaves to the frying pan for the last few minutes of cooking and remove when crisp.

- Meanwhile, toast the cut side of the rolls. When the sausages are ready, put them in the rolls with the rocket and sage leaves and serve immediately.

TOP TIP
A toasted ciabatta would work equally well with this recipe.

Rosemary-roasted Sweet Potatoes

SERVES 4

PREPARATION TIME 5 MINUTES

COOKING TIME 35 MINUTES

INGREDIENTS

2 large sweet potatoes, halved
3 tbsp olive oil
a few sprigs of rosemary
salt and black pepper

METHOD

- Preheat the oven to 190°C (170°C fan) / 375F / gas 5.
- Arrange the potatoes cut side up in a roasting tin. Drizzle with oil and top with the rosemary, then season well with salt and pepper.
- Roast for 35 minutes or until a skewer will slide easily into the centre.

TOP TIP

Use flaked sea salt and freshly ground black pepper for more depth of seasoning.

Tomatoes Stuffed with Herb Risotto

SERVES 16

PREPARATION TIME 15 MINUTES

COOKING TIME 45 MINUTES

INGREDIENTS

1 litre / 1 pint 15 fl. oz / 4 cups good quality
    vegetable stock
2 tbsp olive oil
1 onion, finely chopped
2 cloves of garlic, crushed
150 g / 5 ½ oz / ¾ cup risotto rice
50 g / 1 ¾ oz / ½ cup Parmesan, finely grated
2 tbsp butter
1 tbsp flat leaf parsley, chopped
1 tbsp chives, chopped
1 tbsp thyme leaves
16 large tomatoes
salt and freshly ground black pepper

METHOD

- Heat the stock in a saucepan, keeping it just below simmering point.

- Heat the olive oil in a sauté pan and gently fry the onion for 5 minutes without browning. Add the garlic and cook for 2 more minutes then stir in the rice. When it is well coated with the oil, add 2 ladles of the hot stock. Cook, stirring occasionally, until most of the stock has been absorbed before adding the next 2 ladles. Continue in this way for around 15 minutes or until the rice is just tender.

- Preheat the oven to 190°C (170°C fan) / 375F / gas 5.

- Stir the Parmesan, butter and herbs into the risotto and season with salt and pepper. Cover the pan and take off the heat to rest for 4 minutes.

- Meanwhile, slice the tops off the tomatoes and scoop out the seeds. Arrange them in a baking dish. Beat the risotto really well, then season to taste with salt and pepper. Spoon the risotto into the tomato hollows, then replace the tops.

- Bake the tomatoes for 20 minutes or until tender.

TOP TIP
Replace the thyme leaves with freshly chopped sage or rosemary.

Potato Salad

SERVES 6–8

PREPARATION TIME 10 MINUTES

INGREDIENTS

500 g / 1 lb 5 oz / 4 cups cooked roast
    potatoes, chopped
1 small cucumber, split in half and cut
    into slices
2 tbsp olive oil
salt and freshly ground black pepper
a small bunch of chives, snipped

METHOD

- Combine the roast potatoes, cucumber and olive oil in a large mixing bowl.
- Mix thoroughly until the edges of the potatoes start to soften and turn creamy in appearance.
- Season with plenty of salt and pepper, then spoon into a serving dish.
- Garnish with a sprinkle of chopped chives.

TOP TIP
You could also use cooked new potatoes instead of roast potatoes.

BOXING DAY

Winter Vegetable Salad

SERVES 4

PREPARATION TIME 15 MINUTES

COOKING TIME 15–20 MINUTES

INGREDIENTS

100 g / 3 ½ oz / 1 cup Parmesan, grated
1 medium celeriac, peeled and cubed
2 tbsp white wine vinegar
1 tsp Dijon mustard
1 tsp honey
salt and freshly ground black pepper
110 ml / 4 fl. oz / ½ cup olive oil
300 g / 10 ½ oz / 6 cups baby spinach, washed
100 g / 3 ½ oz / ⅔ cup dried cranberries

METHOD

- Preheat the oven to 180°C (160°C fan) / 350F / gas 4.
- Line a baking tray with a sheet of greaseproof paper and sprinkle the Parmesan onto the paper in four even piles.
- Smooth and shape the piles into rough rectangle shapes.
- Bake for 5–6 minutes until golden and crisp. Remove and leave to cool to one side on a wire rack.
- Cook the celeriac in a large saucepan of salted, boiling water for 8–10 minutes until tender to the point of a knife.
- Drain and leave to cool to one side.
- Whisk together the white wine vinegar, mustard and honey with a little seasoning in a small mixing bowl.
- Gradually add the oil, whisking constantly, until the dressing thickens and emulsifies.
- Add the spinach leaves to a large mixing bowl and add tablespoons of the dressing, tossing well to coat evenly.
- Divide between serving bowls and add the celeriac to the mixing bowl, stirring with a little more dressing if needed.
- Season with salt and pepper, then spoon over the spinach, adding the cranberries on top. Serve with the Parmesan crisps on the side.

TOP TIP
Rocket (arugula) leaves would work equally well in this salad.

Trifle

METHOD

- Combine the caster sugar, water and 150 g / 5 oz / 1 cup of the raspberries in a saucepan.
- Cook over a low heat until the sugar dissolves, then continue to cook for 3 minutes.
- Blitz the mixture in a food processor until smooth, straining the purée through a sieve into a saucepan. Place back over a low heat.
- Soak the gelatine in a small bowl of water until softened. Squeeze out the excess water before adding to the raspberry purée.
- Cook until the gelatine has dissolved, stirring from time to time.
- Place the remaining raspberries in a square pudding dish and pour over the raspberry jelly mixture, then cover and chill for 2 hours until set.
- Once the jelly is set, soak the sponge fingers in the sherry and layer them on top of the jelly. Spoon over the custard and smooth with the back of a tablespoon.
- Whip the cream with the icing sugar and vanilla extract until it forms soft peaks.
- Spread the cream over the custard, then smooth the top with a wet palette knife or tablespoon.
- Garnish with a sprinkle of crushed biscuits and serve.

SERVES 6

PREPARATION TIME 2 HRS 20 MINUTES

COOKING TIME 15 MINUTES

INGREDIENTS

110 g / 4 oz / ½ cup caster (superfine) sugar

250 ml / 9 fl. oz / 1 cup cold water

250 g / 9 oz / 2 cups raspberries

3 sheets of gelatine

12 savoiardi sponge fingers

110 ml / 4 fl. oz / ½ cup cream sherry

450 g / 1 lb / 2 cups ready-made custard

250 ml / 9 fl. oz / 1 cup double (heavy) cream

65 g / 2 ½ oz / ½ cup icing (confectioners') sugar, sifted

½ tsp vanilla extract

2 ginger nut biscuits, crushed

TOP TIP

Add some extra fresh raspberries to the top of your trifle to serve.

Bread and Butter Pudding

SERVES 8
PREPARATION TIME 45 MINUTES
COOKING TIME 30–40 MINUTES

INGREDIENTS

75 g / 3 oz / ⅓ cup unsalted butter, softened
8 slices white sandwich loaf, stale
150 g / 5 oz / 1 cup raisins
1 tsp ground cinnamon
450 ml / 16 fl. oz / 2 cups whole milk
2 medium eggs
65 g / 2 ½ oz / ¼ cup caster (superfine) sugar
icing (confectioners') sugar, to garnish

METHOD

- Lightly grease a rectangular baking dish with a little of the butter, then spread the slices of bread with the remaining butter.

- Place a layer of bread, buttered-side up, in the base of the dish, then add a layer of raisins.

- Sprinkle with a little cinnamon, then repeat the layers of bread and raisins, sprinkling with cinnamon, until all the bread is used.

- Finish with a layer of bread and set the dish to one side.

- Gently warm the milk in a saucepan set over a medium heat until it approaches boiling point, removing it from the heat just before it reaches boiling point.

- Beat the eggs with three-quarters of the sugar until pale and frothy.

- Whisk in the warm milk, then pour the custard over the bread layers, sprinkling with the remaining sugar.

- Leave the pudding to stand for 30 minutes and preheat the oven to 180°C (160°C fan) / 350F / gas 4.

- Bake for 30–40 minutes, until the custard has set and the top is golden brown.

- Remove from the oven and sift a little icing sugar over the top before serving.

TOP TIP
Serve with double (heavy) cream, warm custard or an ice cream of your choice!

Peach and Ginger Crumble

SERVES 4

PREPARATION TIME 15 MINUTES

COOKING TIME 40 MINUTES

INGREDIENTS

4 peaches, peeled, stoned and sliced
75 g / 2 ½ oz / ⅓ cup butter
50 g / 1 ¾ oz / ⅓ cup plain (all-purpose) flour
25 g / 1 oz / ¼ cup ground almonds
2 tsp ground ginger
40 g / 1 ½ oz / ¼ cup light brown sugar

METHOD

- Preheat the oven to 180°C (160°C fan) / 350F / gas 4.
- Arrange the peaches in an even layer in a baking dish.
- Rub the butter into the flour and stir in the ground almonds, ground ginger and sugar. Take a handful of the topping and squeeze it into a clump, then crumble it over the fruit.
- Repeat with the rest of the crumble mixture then bake for 45 minutes or until the topping is golden brown.

TOP TIP
For added crunch, add a handful of chopped hazelnuts (cobnuts) to the crumble.

New
Year's Day

Winter Minestrone

SERVES 6

PREPARATION TIME 5 MINUTES

COOKING TIME 20 MINUTES

INGREDIENTS

2 tbsp olive oil

1 onion, finely chopped

1 carrot, diced

1 celery stick, diced

1 tbsp rosemary, chopped

2 cloves of garlic, finely chopped

2 rashers streaky bacon, chopped

1.2 litres / 2 pints / 4 ¾ cups vegetable stock

150 g / 5 ½ oz / 1 ½ cups dried ditalini or
    similar pasta shapes

400 g / 14 oz / 2 cups canned tomatoes, chopped

3 tbsp Parmesan, grated

METHOD

- Heat the oil in a large saucepan and fry the onion, carrot and celery for 5 minutes without browning. Add the rosemary, garlic and bacon and fry for 2 more minutes.

- Pour in the stock and bring to the boil, then add the pasta and cook for 10 minutes or until al dente.

- Stir in the canned tomatoes and return to the boil, then ladle into warm bowls and sprinkle with Parmesan.

TOP TIP
Serve in hollowed-out bread loaves for a traditional, warming meal.

Stuffed Chicken Legs with Root Vegetables

SERVES 4

PREPARATION TIME 30 MINUTES

COOKING TIME 45 MINUTES

INGREDIENTS

4 chicken legs

200 g / 7 oz / 1 cup baby carrots, peeled

4 small parsnips, peeled and quartered

150 g / 5 ½ oz / 1 cup Jerusalem artichokes,
    peeled and halved

1 garlic bulb, halved horizontally

3 tbsp olive oil

salt and black pepper

FOR THE STUFFING

2 tbsp butter

2 shallots, finely chopped

1 garlic clove, crushed

50 g / 1 ¾ oz / ⅔ cup fresh breadcrumbs

1 tbsp flat leaf parsley, finely chopped

2 cooking chorizo

METHOD

- First make the stuffing: heat the butter in a frying pan and fry the shallots and garlic for 4 minutes or until softened but not brown. Take the pan off the heat and stir in the breadcrumbs and parsley. Skin the chorizo and crumble the meat into the stuffing, then mix well and season with salt and pepper. Leave to cool.

- Preheat the oven to 220°C (200°C fan) / 430F / gas 7.

- Carefully slide your fingers between the skin and flesh of the thighs to create a pocket for the stuffing. Pack the stuffing inside the pocket and flatten it down with the palm of your hand. Close the ends with cocktail sticks.

- Mix the carrots, parsnips, Jerusalem artichokes and garlic together in a roasting tin and lay the chicken quarters on top. Drizzle with olive oil and season with salt and pepper.

- Transfer the tin to the oven and immediately reduce the temperature to 190°C (170°C fan) / 375F / gas 5.

- Roast the chicken for 45 minutes or until the juices run clear when the thickest part is pierced with a skewer.

TOP TIP

Chicken thighs can also be used for a cheaper but equally delicious dish.

Beef Wellington

SERVES 8

PREPARATION TIME 1 HOUR

COOKING TIME 35 MINUTES

INGREDIENTS

750 g / 1 lb 7 oz / 3 cups beef fillet

4 tbsp olive oil

2 tbsp butter

1 large onion, finely chopped

3 cloves of garlic, crushed

2 tbsp fresh thyme leaves

300 g / 10 ½ oz / 2 cups mushrooms, finely chopped

450 g / 1 lb / 1 ½ cups all-butter puff pastry

1 egg, beaten

salt and black pepper

METHOD

- Trim the beef of any sinew, then season well with sea salt and black pepper. Heat half of the oil in a large frying pan until smoking hot, then sear the beef on all sides until nicely browned. Leave to cool.

- Add the rest of the oil and the butter to the pan and turn the heat down to medium. Fry the onion for 5 minutes until translucent, then add the garlic and thyme and cook for another minute, stirring all the time.

- Add the mushrooms and a pinch of salt and cook for 10 minutes or until the liquid that comes out has completely evaporated. Season to taste, then leave to cool. Blend to a smooth purée in a food processor.

- Preheat the oven to 230°C (210°C fan) / 450F / gas 8. Roll out the pastry on a floured surface into a large rectangle. Spread over the mushroom mixture, then sit the beef on top and enclose in the pastry. Crimp the edges and trim away any excess pastry, then brush with beaten egg.

- Bake for 35 minutes or until the pastry is golden and cooked underneath.

TOP TIP

Try to ensure the pastry is well-sealed before cooking for best results.

Roast Beef with Carrots

SERVES 6

PREPARATION TIME 15 MINUTES

COOKING TIME 1 HOUR 30 MINUTES

INGREDIENTS

1.5 kg / 3 lb 3 oz / 8 cups beef sirloin joint

2 tbsp olive oil

2 cloves of garlic

4 carrots, cut into long wedges

2 parsnips, cut into long wedges

a few sprigs of thyme

salt and black pepper

METHOD

- Preheat the oven to 180°C (160°C fan) / 350F / gas 4 and season the beef well with salt and pepper.

- Heat the oil in a frying pan and sear the beef on all sides.

- Mix the garlic, carrots, parsnips and thyme in a baking dish, then sit the beef on top. Transfer to the oven and roast for 1 hour 30 minutes.

- Transfer the beef to a warm plate and leave to rest for 15 minutes before carving, keeping the vegetables warm in a low oven.

TOP TIP

Glaze the vegetables with a drizzle of honey before roasting.

T-bone Steaks with Garlic Butter

SERVES 2

PREPARATION TIME 5 MINUTES

COOKING TIME 15 MINUTES

INGREDIENTS

sunflower oil for deep-frying
4 medium potatoes, cut into wedges
2 T-bone steaks
2 tbsp butter, softened
1 clove of garlic, crushed
1 tbsp flat leaf parsley, finely chopped
salad leaves to serve
salt and freshly ground black pepper

METHOD

- Preheat the grill to its highest setting and heat the oil in a deep fat fryer, according to the manufacturer's instructions, to a temperature of 130°C.

- Lower the potato wedges in the fryer basket and cook for 10 minutes so that they cook all the way through but don't brown.

- Pull up the fryer basket and increase the fryer temperature to 190°C. When the oil has come up to temperature, lower the fryer basket and cook the wedges for 5 minutes or until crisp and golden brown.

- While the wedges are cooking, season the steaks with salt and pepper and grill for 4 minutes on each side or until cooked to your liking. Leave to rest somewhere warm while you finish the wedges.

- Mix the butter with the garlic and parsley, then shape into 2 butter pats.

- Top each steak with a garlic butter pat and serve with the wedges and salad leaves.

TOP TIP
Serve with shop-bought tomato salsa for a simple alteration.

Scallops with Lemon Butter Sauce

SERVES 2

PREPARATION TIME 10 MINUTES

COOKING TIME 8 MINUTES

INGREDIENTS

50 g / 1 ¾ oz / ¼ cup butter, softened
1 lemon, juiced and zest thinly pared
2 tbsp flat leaf parsley, shredded
10 fresh scallops, shelled
black pepper

METHOD

- Preheat the oven to 220°C (200°C fan) / 425F / gas 7.
- Mix the butter with the lemon zest and half the parsley, then season with black pepper.
- Arrange the scallops in a single layer in a snug baking dish and dot the butter over the top.
- Roast the scallops for 8 minutes or until golden brown, with still a trace of translucency in the centres.
- Divide the scallops between two warm bowls. Whisk the lemon juice and the rest of the parsley into the cooking butter, then spoon it over the scallops, before serving.

TOP TIP
This dish is delicious served with warm, crusty bread to mop up the tangy sauce.

Roasted Langoustines with Garlic Butter

SERVES 1

PREPARATION TIME 40 MINUTES

COOKING TIME 8 MINUTES

INGREDIENTS

3 live langoustines
1 tbsp butter, softened
½ clove of garlic, crushed
½ tbsp chervil, finely chopped

METHOD

- Put the langoustines in the freezer for 30 minutes to send them to sleep.
- Preheat the oven to 180°C (160°C fan) / 355 F / gas 4.
- Cut the langoustines in half lengthways and arrange cut side up in a baking dish.
- Mix the butter with the garlic and chervil and dot it over the top, then roast for 8 minutes or until the flesh has just turned opaque.

TOP TIP
Ask your local fishmonger for advice on preparing shellfish.

Rosemary-roasted Potato Wedges

SERVES 4

PREPARATION TIME 10 MINUTES

COOKING TIME 45 MINUTES

INGREDIENTS

4 tbsp olive oil
800 g / 1 lb 12 oz / 2 cups medium potatoes,
    cut into wedges
2 tbsp rosemary leaves
salt and black pepper

METHOD

- Preheat the oven to 200°C (180°C fan) / 400F / gas 6.
- Put the oil in a large roasting tin and heat in the oven for 5 minutes.
- Carefully tip the potato wedges into the pan and turn to coat in the oil, then season well with salt and black pepper and sprinkle with rosemary.
- Bake the wedges for 45 minutes, turning them every 15 minutes, until golden brown on the outside and fluffy within. Sprinkle with a little more sea salt and serve immediately.

TOP TIP
Add a novelty factor and serve these wedges in individual paper cones.

Beer-battered Onion Rings

SERVES 4

PREPARATION TIME 1 HOUR 45 MINUTES

COOKING TIME 25 MINUTES

INGREDIENTS

1 large onion, peeled
300 ml / 10 ½ fl. oz / 1 ¼ cups milk
200 g / 7 oz / 1 ⅓ cups plain (all-purpose)
2 tbsp olive oil
250 ml / 9 fl. oz / 1 cup pale ale
salt and freshly ground black pepper

METHOD

- Thickly slice the onion, then separate the slices into rings.
- Soak the onion rings in milk for 30 minutes, then drain well and pat dry with kitchen paper.
- Meanwhile, make the batter. Sieve the flour into a bowl then whisk in the oil and ale until smoothly combined. Season with salt and pepper.
- Heat the oil in a deep fat fryer, according to the manufacturer's instructions, to a temperature of 180°C.
- Dip the onion rings in the batter, then drop them straight into the hot oil. Fry for 3 minutes or until crisp and brown, then drain well and tip them into a bowl lined with kitchen paper.
- Serve immediately.

TOP TIP
Try serving with a pot of mayonnaise for dipping.

Roasted Mediterranean Vegetables

SERVES 2

PREPARATION TIME 10 MINUTES

COOKING TIME 8 MINUTES

INGREDIENTS

courgettes (zucchinis), thickly sliced
aubergines (eggplants), halved and
  thickly sliced
red peppers, cut into chunks
tbsp olive oil
salt and black pepper

METHOD

- Preheat the oven to 180°C (160°C fan) / 355F / gas 4.
- Toss the vegetables with the oil in a roasting tin and season with salt and pepper.
- Roast for 40 minutes or until lightly charred in places, stirring halfway through.

TOP TIP

Add a roughly-chopped red onion and a couple of garlic cloves for extra vegetables.

Millefeuille

SERVES 4

PREPARATION TIME 30 MINUTES

COOKING TIME 30 MINUTES

INGREDIENTS

450 g / 1 lb / 2 cups all-butter puff pastry

3 tbsp icing (confectioners') sugar

2 tbsp unsweetened cocoa powder

FOR THE CRÈME PATISSIERE

2 large egg yolks

50 g / 1 ¾ oz / ¼ cup caster (superfine) sugar

2 tbsp plain (all-purpose) flour

2 tbsp cornflour (cornstarch)

1 tsp vanilla extract

225 ml / 8 fl. oz / ¾ cup whole milk

METHOD

- Preheat the oven to 220°C (200°C fan) / 425F / gas 7.

- Roll out the pastry on a lightly floured surface and cut it into 3 identical rectangles.

- Transfer the pastry to a baking tray and prick all over with a fork. Lay a second baking tray on top to weigh it down, then bake for 20 minutes or until the pastry is very crisp.

- Remove the top tray and dust the pastry heavily with icing sugar, then return to the oven for 5 minutes or until the sugar has caramelised. Leave to cool completely.

- To make the crème patissiere, stir the egg yolks, sugar, flours and vanilla extract together in a saucepan, then gradually add the milk.

- Heat the mixture until it starts to boil, stirring all the time, then take off the heat and beat vigorously to remove any lumps. Press a sheet of cling film onto the surface and leave to cool to room temperature.

- Sandwich the pastry sheets together with the crème patissiere and dust the top with cocoa, then cut into slices with a very sharp serrated knife.

TOP TIP

Keep chilled in the fridge if not serving immediately.

Cranachan

SERVES 4

PREPARATION TIME 15 MINUTES

COOKING TIME 5 MINUTES

INGREDIENTS

1 tbsp butter

100 g / 3 ½ oz / 1 cup rolled porridge oats

4 tbsp runny honey

300 ml / 10 ½ fl. oz / 1 ¼ cups double (heavy)
     cream

3 tbsp Scotch whisky

200 g / 7 oz / 1 ⅓ cups raspberries

METHOD

- Heat the butter in a large frying pan then stir in the oats. Stir the oats over a medium heat for 3–4 minutes or until they turn golden. Stir in 2 tbsp of honey and cook until golden brown. Tip the oats into a bowl and leave to cool to room temperature.

- Whisk the cream with the whisky and the rest of the honey until softly whipped but not stiff. Lightly mash half of the raspberries and fold them into the cream.

- Divide the toasted oats between four dessert glasses and top with the raspberry cream.

- Spoon the rest of the raspberries on top and serve immediately.

TOP TIP

Replace the raspberries with chopped strawberries for variation.

Poached Plums

METHOD

- Put the plums in a saucepan with the sugar, apple juice and orange zest.
- Bring slowly to a simmer, then poach gently for 10 minutes or until the plums are tender to the point of a knife.
- Let the plums cool a little, then peel off and discard the skins. Serve warm or chilled.

SERVES 4

PREPARATION TIME 5 MINUTES

COOKING TIME 10 MINUTES

INGREDIENTS

8 plums
50 g / 1 ¾ oz / ¼ cup caster (superfine) sugar
250 ml / 9 fl. oz / 1 cup apple juice
1 orange, zest pared into ribbons

TOP TIP
Serve with ice cream for an indulgent dessert.

More
Winter Roasts

Chilli-glazed Roast Pork Belly

SERVES 4

PREPARATION TIME 2 HOURS 15 MINUTES

COOKING TIME 1 HOUR

INGREDIENTS

4 thick portions pork belly, skin removed
250 ml / 9 fl. oz / 1 cup sweet chilli
    (chili) sauce

METHOD

- Cover the pork with the chilli (chili) sauce and leave to marinate for 2 hours or overnight.
- Preheat the oven to 220°C (200°C fan) / 425F / gas 7.
- Roast the pork belly for 15 minutes, then turn down the heat to 160°C (140°C fan) / 325F / gas 3 and roast for a further 45 minutes.
- Leave to rest for 10 minutes in a warm place before serving.

TOP TIP

For a smoky barbecue aroma, marinate the pork in barbecue sauce before roasting.

Roasted Baby Back Ribs

SERVES 4

PREPARATION TIME 4 HOURS 30 MINUTES

COOKING TIME 3 HOURS

INGREDIENTS

2 tbsp olive oil

1 small onion, grated

3 cloves of garlic, crushed

1 tbsp ginger, finely grated

1 tsp mixed spice

200 ml / 7 fl. oz / ¾ cup tomato passata

200 ml / 7 fl. oz / ¾ cup apple juice

3 tbsp dark brown sugar

1 ½ lemons, juiced

1 tbsp Worcestershire sauce

1 tbsp Dijon mustard

2 racks of baby back pork ribs, quartered

2 tbsp chives, chopped

METHOD

- Heat the oil in a saucepan and fry the onion, garlic and ginger for 3 minutes without browning.

- Stir in the mixed spice then add the passata, apple juice, sugar, lemon juice, Worcestershire sauce and mustard with a large pinch of salt and bring to the boil.

- Turn down the heat and simmer for 10 minutes or until the sauce is thick and smooth.

- Leave the sauce to cool, then brush half of it over the ribs and leave to marinate in the fridge for 4 hours or overnight.

- Preheat the oven to 110°C (90°C fan) / 225F / gas ¼.

- Transfer the ribs to a roasting tin and slow-roast for 3 hours, turning occasionally and basting with the rest of the sauce. Sprinkle with chives and serve.

TOP TIP
Serve with cooked pilau rice or thick-cut chips.

Barbecue Foreshank of Lamb

SERVES 6

PREPARATION TIME 25 MINUTES

COOKING TIME 3 HOURS

INGREDIENTS

2 tbsp olive oil

1 small onion, grated

3 cloves of garlic, crushed

1 tbsp ginger, finely grated

1 tsp mixed spice

200 ml / 7 fl. oz / ¾ cup tomato passata

200 ml / 7 fl. oz / ¾ cup apple juice

3 tbsp dark brown sugar

1 ½ lemons, juiced

1 tbsp Worcestershire sauce

1 tbsp Dijon mustard

6 foreshanks of lamb

corn on the cob, steamed rice and green beans to serve

salt and black pepper

METHOD

- Heat the oil in a saucepan and fry the onion, garlic and ginger for 3 minutes without browning.

- Stir in the mixed spice then add the passata, apple juice, sugar, lemon juice, Worcestershire sauce and mustard with a large pinch of salt and bring to the boil.

- Turn down the heat and simmer for 10 minutes or until the sauce is thick and smooth.

- Leave the sauce to cool, then brush half of it over the foreshanks and leave to marinate in the fridge for 4 hours or overnight.

- Preheat the oven to 110°C (90°C fan) / 225F / gas ¼.

- Transfer the foreshanks to a roasting tin and slow-roast for 3 hours, turning occasionally and basting with the rest of the sauce.

- The foreshanks can be toasted over a hot barbecue for a few minutes to impart a smoky taste or served straight from the oven. Serve with grilled corn on the cob, steamed rice and green beans.

TOP TIP

Melt butter over the corn on the cob for a delicious touch.

Roast Lamb with Lavender

SERVES 4

PREPARATION TIME 2 HOURS

COOKING TIME 1 HOUR 10 MINUTES

INGREDIENTS

3 cloves of garlic, crushed
1 tbsp lavender leaves, finely chopped
3 tbsp olive oil
900 g / 2 lb / 4 ½ cups lamb roasting joint
200 ml / 7 fl. oz / ¾ cup Marsala
2 tsp honey
1 tsp lavender flowers

METHOD

- Mix the garlic, lavender leaves and oil into a paste and season with salt and pepper. Rub the mixture over the lamb and leave to marinate for 2 hours or overnight.

- Preheat the oven to 220°C (200°C fan) / 425F / gas 7.

- Roast the lamb for 25 minutes, then turn the oven down to 190°C (170°C fan) / 375F / gas 5, pour over the Marsala and roast for a further 45 minutes.

- Transfer the lamb to a warm plate and cover with a double layer of foil and a towel. Leave to rest for 15 minutes before carving. Stir the honey and lavender flowers into the pan juices and spoon over the top.

TOP TIP
Use sprigs of rosemary instead of lavender, removing before serving.

Pot-roasted Beef with Vegetables

METHOD

- Preheat the oven to 180°C (160°C fan) / 350F / gas 4 and season the beef well with salt and pepper.

- Heat the oil in a cast iron casserole dish and sear the beef on all sides. Remove the beef from the pan then fry the garlic, carrot and celery for 5 minutes. Return the beef to the pot, then pour in the stock and bring to a simmer.

- Put on a lid, transfer it to the oven and pot-roast for 45 minutes.

- Remove the lid, add the tomato and return to the oven for 15 minutes.

- Leave to rest for 10 minutes before carving.

SERVES 8

PREPARATION TIME 15 MINUTES

COOKING TIME 1 HOUR

INGREDIENTS

1.5 kg / 3 lb 3 oz / 8 cups beef sirloin joint
3 tbsp olive oil
4 cloves of garlic, roughly chopped
3 carrots, diced
1 celery stick, cut into short lengths
300 ml / 10 ½ fl. oz / 1 ¼ cups good quality beef stock
1 tomato, quartered
salt and black pepper

TOP TIP

Use large vine tomatoes if available, and add more than one if preferred.

Slow-roasted Brisket with Tomatoes

SERVES 6–8

PREPARATION TIME 25 MINUTES

COOKING TIME 5 HOURS 30 MINUTES

INGREDIENTS

2 tbsp butter
1 onion, finely chopped
2 cloves of garlic, crushed
75 g / 2 ½ oz / 1 cup fresh breadcrumbs
2 tbsp thyme leaves
2.5 kg / 5 ½ lb beef brisket
2 tbsp olive oil
6–8 small tomato vines
salt and freshly ground black pepper

METHOD

- Heat the butter in a frying pan and fry the onion and garlic with a big pinch of salt for 5 minutes or until softened, but not brown. Take the pan off the heat and stir in the breadcrumbs and thyme. Leave to cool.

- Preheat the oven to 200°C (180°C fan) / 400F / gas 6. Unroll the beef brisket, then lay the stuffing in a line down the middle. Roll it back up and tie securely along the length with butchers' string.

- Rub the brisket all over with oil and season with salt and pepper, then transfer it to a shallow roasting tin and roast for 30 minutes.

- Reduce the oven to 140°C (120°C fan) / 275F / gas 1 and cover the brisket loosely with foil. Roast for 3 hours, basting every hour.

- Remove the foil and arrange the tomato vines around the outside of the beef, then return to the oven for 2 hours or until the beef is tender and the tomatoes are starting to collapse.

- Cover the roasting tin and leave to rest somewhere warm for 30 minutes before carving into thick slices.

TOP TIP
Serve with mashed swede and French beans.

Lemon and Rosemary Chicken with Root Vegetables

SERVES 4

PREPARATION TIME 15 MINUTES

COOKING TIME 1 HOUR 10 MINUTES

INGREDIENTS

450 g / 1 lb small / 1 cup rainbow carrots, scrubbed and halved

450 g / 1 lb / 1 cup rainbow beetroot, scrubbed and halved

450 g / 1 lb / 1 cup small potatoes, halved or quartered

2 large sweet potatoes, peeled and cut into large chunks

1.5 kg / 3 lb 5 oz chicken

3 tbsp olive oil

1 lemon, halved

1 tbsp rosemary leaves

1 tbsp thyme leaves

salt and black pepper

METHOD

- Preheat the oven to 200°C (180°C fan) / 400F / gas 6.

- Arrange the vegetables in a large roasting tin. Season the chicken all over with sea salt and black pepper, then sit it on top of the roots and drizzle with olive oil. Squeeze over the lemon halves, then put them inside the cavity. Scatter the herbs over the top.

- Cover the chicken loosely with foil, transfer the tin to the oven and roast for 30 minutes.

- Turn the oven down to 160°C (140°C fan) / 325F / gas 3 and discard the foil. Pour any juices that have collected inside the chicken onto the vegetables and stir them to coat, then put the chicken back on top and roast for a further 40 minutes.

- To test if the chicken is cooked, insert a skewer into the thickest part of the thigh. If the juices run clear with no trace of blood, it is ready. If not, return the chicken to the oven for another 10 minutes and test again.

- Leave the chicken to rest for 10 minutes loosely covered with foil before serving.

TOP TIP

Add parsnips to the roasted vegetables, or red onions for variety.

Roast Bream with Spicy Asparagus Sauce

SERVES 2

PREPARATION TIME 15 MINUTES

COOKING TIME 30 MINUTES

INGREDIENTS

1 large sea bream, gutted and scaled,
    head removed
4 thin slices of lemon
1 tbsp sunflower oil
8 asparagus spears, sliced
3 small dried red chillies (chilies)
2 tbsp saké
2 tbsp rice wine vinegar
1 tbsp runny honey
2 tsp light soy sauce

METHOD

- Preheat the oven to 220°C (200°C fan) / 430F / gas 7. Make 2 deep incisions down each side of the fish and stuff each one with a piece of lemon.

- Lay the fish in a roasting tin and roast for 30 minutes or until the flesh comes away from the bone easily in the thickest part.

- Meanwhile, heat the oil in a wok and stir-fry the asparagus and chillies for 3 minutes. Pour in the saké, vinegar, honey and soy and bubble until slightly thickened.

- Spoon the asparagus sauce over the bream and serve.

TOP TIP
Use a warm spoon to
pour the honey.

Roast Dinner Gravy

SERVES 6

PREPARATION TIME 5 MINUTES

COOKING TIME 2 HOURS 15 MINUTES

INGREDIENTS

450 g / 1 lb / 3 cups chicken wings and giblets
    or bones and meat trimmings from the joint
1 onion, halved
1 carrot, chopped
1 celery stick, chopped
8 black peppercorns
2 bay leaves
2 tbsp plain (all-purpose) flour
roasting juices from the chicken or
    meat joint

METHOD

- Put the chicken wings and giblets or bones and meat trimmings from the joint in a saucepan with the onion, carrot, celery, peppercorns and bay leaves. Add enough cold water to cover everything by 5 cm (2 in), then bring the pan to a gentle simmer.

- Simmer the stock very gently for 1–2 hours or for the duration of the roasting time, adding a little more water if it starts to run low.

- When the chicken or joint is ready, transfer it to a warm plate and cover with a double layer of foil and a towel to rest. Strain the stock through a sieve into a jug.

- Put the roasting tin over a medium heat on the hob and bring the pan juices to the boil. Stir in the flour, then gradually incorporate the hot stock, stirring all the time. Bring to a simmer and stir until the gravy has thickened slightly. Season to taste with salt and pepper, then pour it into a warmed gravy jug.

TOP TIP
Gravy can be frozen and used at a later date.

Festive Bakes

Christmas Cake

SERVES 12
PREPARATION TIME 30–35 MINUTES
COOKING TIME 3 HOURS 45–55 MINUTES

INGREDIENTS

750 g / 1 lb 10 oz / 5 cups mixed dried fruit
    (raisins, currants, sultanas)
100 g / 3 ½ oz / ⅔ cup glacé cherries, chopped
250 ml / 9 fl. oz / 1 cup stout
75 ml / 3 fl. oz / ⅓ cup dark rum
1 orange, zested
2 tbsp treacle
225 g / 8 oz / 1 cup unsalted butter, softened
225 g / 8 oz / 1 ⅓ cups dark brown soft sugar
250 g / 9 oz / 1 ⅔ cup plain (all-purpose)
    flour, sifted
1 tsp baking powder
5 medium eggs, beaten
1 tsp ground allspice
½ tsp ground nutmeg
75 g / 3 oz / ¾ cup ground almonds
250 g / 9 oz / 1 ¼ cups marzipan
a little icing (confectioners') sugar, for dusting
2 tbsp apricot jam (jelly), warmed
300 g / 10 ½ oz / 1 ⅓ cups white fondant icing
2 tbsp green fondant icing
marzipan fruits, to garnish
silver dragée balls, to garnish

METHOD

- Preheat the oven to 150°C (130°C fan) / 300F / gas 2 and grease and line a 20 cm (8 in) round cake tin with greaseproof paper.

- Combine the mixed dried fruit, glacé cherries, stout, rum, orange zest and treacle in a large saucepan.

- Cook over a low heat for 10 minutes, stirring occasionally, then remove the mixture from the heat and leave to cool to one side.

- Combine the butter, sugar, flour, baking powder, eggs, spices and almonds in a large mixing bowl and beat thoroughly for 2–3 minutes until smooth.

- Fold the fruit mixture from the saucepan into the batter and spoon into the prepared tin. Smooth the top with a wet tablespoon or palette knife and bake for 3 hours.

- Check the cake and cover the top with a round of greaseproof paper. Bake for another 45–55 minutes until a cake tester comes out clean when inserted in the centre of the cake.

- Remove the cake to a wire rack to cool. Once cool, turn out the cake and trim the top with a serrated knife so that it is flat.

- Roll out the marzipan on a surface dusted with icing sugar to 1 cm (½ in) thickness. Brush the cake with apricot jam and drape the marzipan over it, pressing to stick, and trimming to fit.

- Roll out the fondant icing to approximately the same thickness as the marzipan, then brush the marzipan with warmed water and drape the icing over it. Press well to seal, trimming the edges as necessary for a clean finish.

- Roll out the green fondant and cut into leaf shapes. Sit the leaves on top of the cake and garnish with marzipan fruits and dragée balls before serving.

Mince Pies

MAKES 24

PREPARATION TIME 55–60 MINUTES

COOKING TIME 15–20 MINUTES

INGREDIENTS

225 g / 8 oz / 1 cup unsalted butter, softened

125 g / 4 ½ oz / 1 cup icing (confectioners')
    sugar, plus extra for dusting

2 medium egg yolks

275 g / 10 oz / 1 ¾ cups plain (all-purpose)
    flour, plus extra for dusting

400 g / 14 oz / 2 cups mincemeat

1 medium egg, beaten

METHOD

- Beat the butter in a mixing bowl until pale and creamy, then sift in the icing sugar and beat until well combined.

- Beat in the egg yolks until blended, then sift in the flour, mixing to a dough.

- Knead lightly until smooth, then wrap in cling film and chill for 30 minutes.

- Preheat the oven to 200°C (180°C fan) / 400F / gas 6.

- Grease a 24-hole mini muffin or cupcake tin.

- Divide the dough in half and roll out each half on a lightly floured surface to 5 mm (¼ in) thickness.

- Cut out 24 rounds to fit the tins from one half and cut out 24 stars with a smaller star-shaped cutter from the other half.

- Line the holes of the prepared tin with the rounds of pastry and fill with mincemeat.

- Top with the pastry stars and brush with beaten egg. Bake for about 15 minutes until the pastry is golden and the mincemeat is bubbling.

- Remove from the oven and leave to cool for 10 minutes, then move to a wire rack to cool completely.

- Turn out and sift a little icing sugar over the tops before serving.

TOP TIP

Different shapes can be used for the tops of the pies.

Chocolate Yule Log

SERVES 8

PREPARATION TIME 45–50 MINUTES

COOKING TIME 8–10 MINUTES

INGREDIENTS

225 g / 8 oz / 1 cup caster (superfine) sugar

4 medium eggs

75 g / 3 oz / ½ cup plain (all-purpose)
    flour, sifted

2 tbsp cocoa powder, sifted

2 tbsp brandy

225 ml / 8 fl. oz / 1 cup double (heavy) cream

110 g / 4 oz / ½ cup sweetened chestnut purée

75 g / 3 oz / ½ cup dark chocolate, chopped

85 ml / 3 ½ fl. oz / ⅓ cup water

2 medium egg yolks

110 g / 4 oz / ½ cup unsalted butter, softened

150 g / 5 oz / 1 cup coarsely grated chocolate

icing (confectioners') sugar, to garnish

METHOD

- Preheat the oven to 200°C (180°C fan) / 400F / gas 6. Grease and line a 33 cm x 23 cm (13 in x 9 in) Swiss roll tin.

- Cut a second piece of paper a little larger than the tin and sprinkle with 2 tsp of the caster sugar, setting it to one side.

- Combine 110 g / 4 oz / ½ cup of the sugar with the eggs in a mixing bowl and whisk until pale and frothy. Sift together the flour and cocoa powder and gently fold into the egg mixture, then pour into the tin, tilting it so that it runs evenly over the surface.

- Bake for 8–10 minutes until firm and springy to the touch, then remove to a wire rack to cool.

- Turn out the cooked sponge on to the sugared paper. Peel away the lining paper and trim the edges. Sprinkle the brandy over the sponge and whip the cream until softly peaked.

- Spread the cream over the sponge, dot with chestnut purée and roll it into a cylinder, working from the back edge rolling forward.

- Melt the chocolate in a heatproof bowl set over a half-filled saucepan of simmering water. Stir until melted, then remove to the side.

- Heat the remaining sugar and water in a pan over a low heat until the sugar dissolves. Boil rapidly until syrupy.

- Whisk the egg yolks in a bowl and continue whisking while adding the sugar syrup in a steady stream. Whisk until the mixture becomes thick, pale and cool, leaving a trail on the surface.

- Beat the butter in a separate bowl until soft. Gradually beat in the egg mixture until thick and fluffy, then fold through the melted chocolate.

- Cover the log with the buttercream and press the grated chocolate on the top and sides of the cake. Sift over a little icing sugar just before serving.

Christmas Star Biscuits

MAKES 16

PREPARATION TIME 20 MINUTES

COOKING TIME 12–15 MINUTES

INGREDIENTS

110 g / 4 oz / ½ cup unsalted butter, softened

½ tsp vanilla extract

75 g / 3 oz / ⅓ cup caster (superfine) sugar

2 tbsp light brown sugar

1 medium egg

250 g / 9 oz / 1 ⅔ cups plain (all-purpose) flour

½ tsp salt

½ tsp bicarbonate of (baking) soda

1 tsp ground allspice

½ tsp ground cinnamon

a little plain (all-purpose) flour, for dusting

METHOD

- Preheat the oven to 180°C (160°C fan) / 350°F / gas 4 and grease and line two large baking trays.

- Cream together the butter, vanilla extract and sugars together in a large mixing bowl for 2–3 minutes until pale and smooth. Beat in the egg, mixing well.

- Beat in the flour in thirds, together with the salt, followed by the bicarbonate of soda and spices. Stir at first to incorporate well, but take care not to overwork the dough.

- Roll the dough out to 5 mm (¼ in) thickness on a lightly floured surface and cut into stars using a star-shaped cookie cutter.

- Arrange the stars spaced out on the baking trays and bore a small hole in the top of each.

- Bake for 12–15 minutes until just starting to brown at the edges, then remove to a wire rack to cool.

- Once cool, you can hang the biscuits as decorations using thread or ribbon.

TOP TIP

Seal in confectionery bags and tie with ribbons as gifts. Use within a few days.

Chocolate Christmas Tree

SERVES 8

PREPARATION TIME 15–20 MINUTES

COOKING TIME 25–35 MINUTES

INGREDIENTS

350 g / 12 oz / 1 cup caster (superfine) sugar

350 g / 12 oz / 1 cup margarine, softened

350 g / 12 oz / 1 ¼ cup self-raising flour, sifted

75 g / 3 oz / ¾ cup ground almonds

2 tbsp cocoa powder, sifted

6 large eggs, lightly beaten

55 ml / 2 fl. oz / ¼ cup whole milk

100 g / 3 ½ oz / ⅔ cup chocolate chips

100 g / 3 ½ oz / ¾ cup icing (confectioners') sugar, to dust

METHOD

- Preheat the oven to 180°C (160°C fan) / 350F / gas 4.

- Grease and line a 23 cm (9 in), 18 cm (7 in), 15 cm (6 in) and a 10 cm (4 in) cake tin with greaseproof paper.

- Combine all the ingredients apart from the chocolate chips and icing sugar in a large mixing bowl.

- Beat thoroughly for 3–4 minutes until smooth, then fold through the chocolate chips.

- Divide the mixture between the prepared tins and bake for 25–35 minutes until a cake tester comes out clean from their centres. Remove the sponges to a wire rack to cool.

- Once cool, turn out and trim the tops with a serrated knife until perfectly flat.

- Cut the sponges into star shapes, cutting a small star from any leftover sponge.

- Layer the sponges in tiers, placing the smallest star on its end on top of the cake.

- Dust liberally with icing sugar before serving.

TOP TIP

Dust with cinnamon and icing (confectioners') sugar for a spiced version.

Stollen

SERVES 8

PREPARATION TIME 1 HOUR 45 MINUTES

COOKING TIME 40–45 MINUTES

INGREDIENTS

125 ml / 4 ½ fl. oz / ½ cup whole milk, warmed

2 tsp dried active yeast

250 g / 9 oz / 1 ⅔ cups plain (all-purpose)
    flour, sifted

a pinch of salt

1 tsp ground mixed spice

1 tsp ground cinnamon

1 tbsp caster (superfine) sugar

65 g / 2 ½ oz / ¼ cup unsalted butter, softened

1 large egg, lightly beaten

55 g / 2 oz / ½ cup ground almonds

150 g / 5 oz / 1 cup mixed candied
    peel, chopped

150 g / 5 oz / 1 cup sultanas and/or raisins

a little extra plain (all-purpose) flour, for
    dusting

100 g / 3 ½ oz / ¾ cup icing (confectioners')
    sugar, for dusting

METHOD

- Combine the warmed milk and yeast in a mixing bowl and leave for 5 minutes.
- Mix together the flour, salt, ground spices and sugar in a large mixing bowl. Then add the butter, egg, ground almonds, mixed candied peel and sultanas and/or raisins and mix well.
- Add the milk and yeast mixture to the bowl and stir well until it comes together as a dough.
- Turn the dough out onto a lightly floured surface and knead for 5–6 minutes until even and smooth.
- Cover with a damp tea towel and leave to prove for 20 minutes.
- After proving, knock the dough back and knead again for a further 5 minutes.
- Shape the dough into an elongated oval shape and transfer to a greased baking tray, then cover with a damp tea towel and leave to prove in a warm place for 1 hour.
- Preheat the oven to 180°C (160°C fan) / 350F / gas 4. Bake the stollen for 40–45 minutes until risen and golden on the outside.
- Remove from the oven and transfer to a wire rack to cool. Dredge the stollen with icing sugar before slicing and serving.

TOP TIP

Sprinkle coconut on top of the stollen with icing (confectioners') sugar.

Banana and Cinnamon Pastries

SERVES 4

PREPARATION TIME 30 MINUTES

COOKING TIME 18 MINUTES

INGREDIENTS

450 g / 1 lb / 2 cups puff pastry

100 g / 3 ½ oz / ½ cup dried banana chips

2 ripe bananas, peeled

3 tbsp light brown sugar

½ tsp cinnamon

1 egg, beaten

2 tbsp caster (superfine) sugar

METHOD

- Preheat the oven to 220°C (200°C fan) / 430 F / gas 7.

- Roll the pastry out on a lightly floured surface and cut it into 4 squares.

- Put the banana chips in a plastic sandwich bag, then wrap the bag in a tea towel and crush with a rolling pin. Mash the bananas with a fork, then stir in the crushed banana chips, sugar and cinnamon.

- Spoon a quarter of the mixture in a line down the centre of each pastry square.

- Cut the exposed sides of the pastry into strips on the diagonal, then starting at the top, fold them across, alternating between the two sides as you work your way down.

- Transfer the pastries to a baking parchment-lined baking tray, brush with beaten egg and sprinkle with caster sugar.

- Bake the pastries for 18 minutes or until the pastry is puffy and golden on top and cooked through underneath. Serve warm or at room temperature.

TOP TIP

These pastries are wonderful for an indulgent breakfast.

Chocolate Bundt Cake

SERVES 8

PREPARATION TIME 1 HOUR 25 MINUTES

COOKING TIME 45 MINUTES

INGREDIENTS

225 g / 8 oz / 1 cup butter, softened
225 g / 8 oz / 1 cup caster (superfine) sugar
4 large eggs, beaten
125 g / 4 ½ oz / ¾ cup self-raising flour
100 g / 3 ½ oz / 1 cup ground almonds
3 tbsp unsweetened cocoa powder

TO FINISH

100 g / 3 ½ oz / ¾ cup dark chocolate
    (minimum 60% cocoa solids), chopped
2 tbsp butter
2 tbsp golden syrup

METHOD

- Preheat the oven to 180°C (160°C fan) /
  355F / gas 4 and butter a bundt tin.

- Cream the butter and sugar together until
  well whipped then gradually whisk in the
  eggs, beating well after each addition.

- Fold in the flour, ground almonds and
  cocoa then scrape the mixture into the tin.

- Bake the cake for 45 minutes or until a
  skewer inserted in the centre comes out
  clean. Turn the cake out onto a wire rack
  and leave to cool completely.

- Melt the chocolate, butter and syrup
  together over a low heat, stirring regularly,
  then spoon it over the cake.

TOP TIP

Sprinkle the top with a
few silver dragee balls to
add some sparkle.

Marmalade Breton Gateau

SERVES 6

PREPARATION TIME 15 MINUTES

COOKING TIME 40 MINUTES

INGREDIENTS

250 g / 9 oz / 1 ¼ cups butter, cubed
250 g / 9 oz / 1 ¼ cups plain (all-purpose) flour
250 g / 9 oz / 1 ¼ cups caster (superfine) sugar
5 large egg yolks
175 g / 6 oz / ½ cup marmalade
icing (confectioners') sugar for dusting
pinch of salt

METHOD

- Preheat the oven to 180°C (160°C fan) / 350F / gas 4 and butter a 20 cm (8 in) round loose-bottomed cake tin.

- Rub the butter into the flour with a pinch of salt then stir in the sugar. Beat the egg yolks and stir them into the dry ingredients. Bring the mixture together into a soft dough and divide it in two.

- Put 1 half in the freezer for 10 minutes. Press the other half into the bottom of the cake tin to form an even layer. Spread the marmalade on top. Coarsely grate the other half of the dough over the top and press down lightly.

- Bake the tart for 40 minutes or until golden brown and cooked through.

- Cool completely before unmoulding and dusting with icing sugar.

TOP TIP
Serve with cream or ice cream.

INDEX